ALTERNATIVE WEDDINGS

ALTERNATIVE WEDDINGS

*An Essential Guide for Creating
Your Own Ceremonies*

Jane Ross-Macdonald

Taylor Publishing Company
Dallas, Texas

Published by Taylor Publishing Company
1550 West Mockingbird Lane
Dallas, Texas 75235

First printed in 1996 in the United Kingdom by Thorsons, an imprint of
HarperCollins Publishers.

Book design by Mark McGarry

Library of Congress Catologing-in-Publication Data

Ross-Macdonald, Jane
    Alternative weddings: an essential guide for creating your own
ceremony/ Jane Ross-MacDonald.
        p. cm.
    Includes bibliographical references and index.
    ISBN 0–87833–977–9
    1. Marriage service. 2. Weddings. I. Title.
BL462.R67   1997   97–6649
392.5—dc21   CIP

Printed in the United States of America
10 9 8 7 6 5 4 3 2

For Rupert

Contents

Acknowledgments

I would like to thank the following people who shared details of their weddings with me and gave permission for me to quote from their ceremonies (some of the names have been changed at their request):

Katy and Peter Clement, who married on a beach in Florida and had a nondenominational church blessing one year later;

Roz and Dave Morris, who married in a hotel room in Mexico City;

Robert and Miranda Holden, who had an open-air blessing drawing on a variety of spiritual traditions;

Sarah Carver and Paul Rees, who had a vegetarian reception in a Friends Meeting Hall after a civil ceremony;

Maria Coello and Stephen Newton, who conducted their own pacifist ceremony in a forest;

Alison Vickers and Tim Wainwright, who had a civil service followed by a ceremony of blessing and celebration in Alison's parents' garden;

James Clifton and Sharon Williams, who had a Pagan ceremony on hilltop;

Nicola and Alasdair Saunders, who had a tenth-century Viking-style wedding;

Joanna Webb and Tony Moore, who married in a theater in Australia;

Karen and Lee Chang-Rawlinson, who had a Pagan/lesbian ceremony in a friend's back garden;

Nicola and Pascal Lecerf, who married in the Seychelles islands on an astrologically auspicious day;

Margaret Gregory and Colin Wall, who had a civil service in the presence of their three-week-old son;

Philip and Steve Hawkesford-Curry, who had an evening ceremony based around an adaptation of the Humanist gay "affirmation" ceremony;

Christine Baker and Mark Willis, who had a Humanist celebration;

Christine Kijko, who married her partner, Jim, in a hospital;

Roy Dalgleish and Martin Weaver, who had a celebration of partnership in a castle in the Forest of Dean in the United Kingdom;

Amanda Shribman and Avril Hollings, who held a lesbian commitment ceremony with Pagan, Goddess, Jewish, and Buddhist elements;

Nicola and Humphrey Cobbold, whose wedding combined Jewish and Christian elements;

Janet and John Moorhouse, who held a Buddhist ceremony after a civil wedding;

Nahid Moshtael and Peter Gregory, who had a Baha'i wedding;

Diane Wilkinson and Simon Bebbington, who had a Humanist wedding;

Darcy Twose and Peter Walop, who held a Humanist ceremony in the grounds of a hotel overlooking the sea;

Catherine and Ian Beaumont, who married on a Hawaiian beach;

Sumita Davis and Stewart Maland, who had a Las Vegas wedding;

Jeanette and Jim Kelly, who married in the town hall in Prague;

Karen Kowalske and Jean Morris who had a Christian Holy Union service in Dallas, Texas;

Steve Habgood and Mark Sadlek, who held a Ceremony of Affirmation on their fifth anniversary;

Todd Myers and Michael Gruver, whose ceremony was a "nontraditional, nonreligious, nongender, personal creation;"

Patrick Carroll and Don Solomon, who held a Quaker-inspired ceremony in Hollywood that coincided with the first full moon of the new year;

Michael McLean and Mark Smith, who chose a "semireligious" Unitarian ceremony and held it in a turn of the century mansion in Dallas;

Tymythy Aieran and Norman Hadley, who held a pagan "trysting" ceremony in Norman's backyard in California;

Brian and Karen Gray, who married on Sandals La Toc, St. Lucia.

I'd also like to thank the following people for their help while I was researching the different traditions and ceremonies in this book: George Broadhead, Richard Kirker, Carmen Henry, Sally Spears, the Rev. John Clifford and the Rev. Andrew Hill, Gyles Brandreth MP, Simon Allen,

Acknowledgments

Lawrence Murray, Wendy Tennant, and Mark Rimmer. Finally I'd like to thank Erica Smith, Lisa Eaton, Macy Jaggers and Jason Rath at Taylor Publishing; and all the Ross-Macdonalds, Graham-Maws and Werrys for their unflagging support and occasional musical contributions.

I am indebted to the following for permission to reprint extracts:

Marriage Prayer. © Robert and Miranda Holden.

Six lines from *Weddings from the Heart.* © 1991, Daphne Rose Kingma. Reprinted by permission of Conari Press.

ASB Wedding Service. Reprinted by permission of the Central Board of Finance of the Church of England.

Spiritualist Wedding Ceremony. Reprinted by permission of the Spiritualists' National Union.

Pagan Wedding Ritual. From *Rituals for Everyday Living,* © 1994, Lorna St. Aubyn. Reprinted by permission of Piatkus Books.

Druid Wedding. From *The Druid Way,* © 1993, Philip Carr-Gomm. Reprinted by permission of Element Books.

Seven lines from *To Love and To Cherish,* © 1988, Jane Wynne Willson. Reprinted by permission of the author.

Gay and Lesbian Humanist Ceremony. Reprinted by permission of GALHA.

Preface

Congratulations! Making the decision to spend the rest of your life with someone is a major event in anyone's life. It might be something you have dreamed of ever since you were a small child reading fairy stories. It might be a long-waged campaign to capture the heart of a certain someone, or it might suddenly come upon you with the fierceness of a flash of lightning. For others it is a quieter, calmer sense of "coming home." It is a decision you make as a couple, together: gradually with a dawning sense of realization, or suddenly, passionately, inevitably.

Many couples feel the need to mark this rite of passage with a public celebration rather than drifting into long-term cohabitation and want the ceremony to express their love for each other in a way. Together, perhaps over dinner or walking along a beach, you discuss the kind of wedding you want. Some will opt for the traditional white church wedding, with all the trimmings. Those from different religious backgrounds may follow the traditional Jewish, Hindu, or Muslim ceremony. Others choose the civil ceremony at the courthouse, with perhaps a family lunch afterward.

For a growing number of couples, however, the decision is not so clear cut. If you are not strongly religious and feel a traditional wedding would be hypocritical, if you feel a civil ceremony is rather austere, if you have been married before or are marrying someone from a different culture, if you are gay or lesbian, if your two families are at loggerheads, or if your finances can't stretch to a lavish "do" . . . in short, if you want a different, personal, meaningful wedding that expresses your own view of the world, what can you do?

This book aims to set out the options for creating your own wedding. It looks at various religious and spiritual traditions as well as nonreligious weddings. It explains exactly what the legal issues are, and how much leeway you have in designing your own ceremony and choosing the venue. Covering all the stages from proposal to honeymoon, it will give you ideas for writing your own vows, accompanied by sample services and real-life examples. It will also give you suggestions for readings, music, and venues—whether you want to spice up an otherwise traditional wedding, or go for a completely alternative one.

The possible range of alternative weddings is as rich and varied as your imagination, so inevitably this book does not try to be comprehensive. I hope it will, however, provide you with a good overview of a wide variety of weddings and inspire you to make your own choices.

While I was researching this book, I talked to many couples who had chosen a different style of wedding. These ranged from two people who were married in a hotel room in Mexico (having bribed some officials and dragged a couple of witnesses off the street), through couples who chose tropical islands for their weddings, to couples who wrote their own vows for ceremonies outside a temple or in a forest.

The most important piece of advice these couples offered is to *make your own decisions* and not to be deflected by parents, friends, or relatives from doing what you want. Remember, it is *your* day, *your* wedding, the start of *your* lives together. Create a wedding that is special and sacred for you, that expresses your intentions, wishes, and feelings, and you will find that it will be a joyous and romantic occasion to remember for the rest of your lives.

PART ONE

1

Marriage in the 1990s and Beyond

HUNDREDS of thousands of couples in the United States tie the knot each year, undeterred by the escalating rate of divorce. This fact, as Beatrice Webb noted, is evidence of "the triumph of hope over experience" or—less cynically—proof that romance is alive and well and that people have a fundamental urge to declare their love for each other publicly by making a positive statement of enduring commitment.

These couples are bombarded with advice, magazines, mailings, books, and exhibitions by one huge industry with the sole aim of "making your special day a day to remember"—and of making handsome profits for dressmakers, cake decorators, printers, florists, gift shops, caterers, and a host of others. Every wedding magazine exhorts young brides to buy into the romantic notion of a perfect white wedding, offering "essential" advice on what to wear, what not to wear, how many ushers to have, color schemes, bridesmaids' shoes, long lasting make-up, timing, seating plans—all implying that any departure from the norm would be a dreadful faux pas. It is hardly surprising, then, that it can take up to a year to organize a large traditional wedding—a year that can at best be frenetically busy but at worst can be fraught with heated quarrels, tears, and threats to call it all off.

Stephen (a twenty-nine-year old stockbroker) talks of how he was completely excluded from the wedding arrangements by his bride's mother:

She insisted on doing it all herself: flowers, food, guest list, the lot. She even

3

chose the hymns! I should have been more assertive, I suppose, but I didn't want to cause a fuss. And at first I was pleased not to have to bother with all the details. Suzanne seemed quite happy with the situation, but it did cause problems between the two of us in the run-up to the wedding, and we'd have endless arguments about the tiniest things.

Elizabeth (a twenty-five-year-old actress) had divorced parents. Her father had a new wife and stepchildren and her mother had just divorced from her second husband:

> You wouldn't believe the rows we had over the wording of the invitations. I wanted both my parents to be on it, my mother wanted to use her maiden name and my father didn't want her on it at all! Both wanted the replies to come to them. In the end we had to get two sets printed. Alan and I felt we should have been given awards for services to diplomacy after six months of careful negotiating with each set of parents!

Unless you are very careful, there are many things that can conspire against the two most important people: the bride and groom. Instead of your wedding being a special, personal event, it becomes a public pageant of inestimable cost, complicated by an assortment of friends and relatives offering well-meant but intrusive advice. As Vivienne (a thirty-three-year-old fashion journalist) said:

> By the time we got to the wedding day itself, we had almost forgotten why we were doing it. I consider myself a sensible, well-adjusted, thoughtful person, but even I became consumed by worries about buttonholes, royal icing, and marquee swags. It wasn't until our quiet honeymoon on the Isle of Skye that we felt really married, in the spiritual sense.

Clara (a twenty-two-year-old secretary), who was planning a traditional white wedding—huge train, marquee, two hundred guests at the church ("the works")—described her reaction after seeing the film *Four Weddings and a Funeral*:

> I can't see why everyone thought it was such a hilarious film. It felt like my plans for a dream wedding had been ripped to shreds. It made me see how boring and how samey church weddings are. Now I'm determined to do something different, even if it's only having a twenties theme, chocolate cake, and leaving by hot-air balloon!

These are, if you like, the negative reasons for not going down the aisle in white. But quite apart from the fuss and bother of a traditional wedding, couples are starting to want to do things their own way. No longer feeling straight-jacketed by convention, pulling away from organized religion, and experimenting with new ideas, people are searching out their own directions. Ostentation is out, simplicity is in, as the materialism of the 1980s gives way to a new individuality and sense of spirituality. Marriage is not socially essential these days, so people are thinking very carefully about why they are doing it and what it means for them. The very idea of marriage is changing, just as it has evolved through several incarnations over thousands of years. If you are considering doing it differently, you are at the cutting edge of this trend!

WHY AN ALTERNATIVE WEDDING?

In America, "land of freedom," the choices for a alternative wedding are as rich and varied as your imagination. In many other countries—such as the UK—the law is still very restrictive in terms of what you may and may not do. Still, in the United States, as elsewhere, there are traditionalists and there are those who want (or need) to break free of the shackles of convention. We tend to think of alternative weddings as those in unusual venues: up a mountain, in a hot air balloon, over the Internet, and so on. But the reality goes much further than this. Couples are thinking deeply about the kind of service they want, about what it says about their relationship and how it reflects their beliefs and lifestyles. There are many reasons couples choose to do things their own way. Here are some I came across from speaking to the people who contributed to this book.

Lack of religious conviction. The overriding reasons for rejecting a traditional wedding are usually religious ones. If you don't believe in God, what is the point of making vows and promises within a religious context, the argument goes. Todd (a twenty-two-year-old registered nurse) and Michael (a thirty-five-year-old attorney) designed their own ceremony to reflect their equality and to express their atheism and agnosticism. Says Todd, "we wanted no expression of traditional Christian views to play a part in our ceremony. I didn't and don't want any sort of permission from any religious organization to 'sanctify' my love or commitment to Michael."

Patriarchal and sexist symbolism. Quite apart from the fervent wish of most modern brides never to utter the word "obey" as part of their wedding vows, many church ceremonies are charged with overtones that many women, and increasingly men, find hard to reconcile with their lifestyles and attitudes. The woman, dressed in virginal white, modestly veiled, is handed over by her father or another male to her new husband. Things are done *to* her, rather than *by* her: "I didn't want to be given away—I'm not a parcel!" commented Katy (a twenty-one-year-old student). The emphasis is also on the procreation of children, whether you want to have them or not—whether you are able to have them or not. Roz (a twenty-seven-year-old journalist), said:

> I didn't want such a personally important occasion to be put in a religious context (with its "marriage is created by God for the creation of children" business) when what was important was that I was making a commitment to a person.

The need to personalize the service. When you stand up to make your vows before witnesses, you want to convey your feelings truly and sincerely—your signature needs to be on the whole day. The couples I spoke to wanted the service to express who they were and why they were marrying. Many wanted to say more than was possible with the standard wedding service, and to make it more personal. "Your wedding day is the most authentic day of your life. If you aren't true to yourself then, when can you be?" asked Robert (a twenty-five-year-old writer and psychologist), while Sarah (a twenty-six-year-old social worker) and Paul (a twenty-nine-year-old child psychiatrist) felt, "We didn't want to be hypocrites on such an important day (or ever!)"

Maria (a twenty-five-year-old teacher) and Stephen (a twenty-four-year-old teacher), who devised their own ceremony and held it in a forest, said:

> We wanted our wedding to be a celebration of the type of people we are, so it was important that our common beliefs and values were a part of that celebration. If we'd had a traditional wedding it would not have said anything about our relationship with each other.

Decide what values you want your wedding to embody, and you will find the service will fall into place. Said Alison (a twenty-nine-year-old campaign director for Amnesty International):

> We wanted a wedding that both we and our friends felt comfortable with. We were committed to a ceremony in which we played equal roles and that could have been equally relevant to our gay friends. We wanted to get married in a beautiful place (my parents' garden) and have a sense of space and light and celebration.

Weddings certainly can be dull. One summer I went to nine traditional church weddings. They have all now merged in my mind—a fact I put down to the similarity of the proceedings rather than the quantity of champagne I consumed. Roz and Dave (a thirty-five-year-old author), who married in Mexico, insisted, "We wanted a personal, unique wedding, not a rerun of a ceremony everyone has seen hundreds of times."

A desire for celebration and romance over solemnity. Traditional services can sometimes be over-formal, sacrificing joy and romance at the altar of respectability. By creating your own ceremony and choosing where to get married—whether it's a beautiful European city or in a canoe on a mountain lake—you can inject enthusiasm and happiness without feeling boring and conventional. After all, you will (ideally) never get married again, so you might as well make sure you have fun on the day. James (a twenty-five-year-old hairdresser) and Sharon (a twenty-nine-year-old Reiki Master and therapist), who met on an ashram in Goa, opted for a nonlegal ceremony on Glastonbury Tor in the United Kingdom. "A lot of people are put off by marriage itself," they said. "It wasn't that we particularly wanted not to conform, but we felt religious weddings were too fanatical and didn't convey enough love."

Spirituality as opposed to Christianity. I spoke to several couples who firmly assured me that they were deeply spiritual people but who nevertheless could not find anything in Christianity that answered their needs or reflected their beliefs in a meaningful way. These are people who refused to compromise with a church wedding, despite the temptations of solemnity and grandeur. Maria and Stephen commented:

> Neither of us assigns ourself to a particular denomination or its inherent values. However, we do believe in some type of universal power. We wanted

7

our celebration to include the essence of marriage from all faiths, for every faith seems to teach that what you give out you get back. Having both experienced multiculturalism in different ways in our lives, we wanted everyone to feel comfortable at our wedding, no matter what their faith or background.

"Neither of us has any religious or spiritual convictions," said Nicola (a twenty-seven-year-old technical writer) and Alasdair (a twenty-six-year-old civil servant), "and we are both fascinated by Viking society." Naturally enough, their wedding was designed according to a tenth-century Viking ceremony.

Joanna (a twenty-nine-year-old actress) and Tony (a forty-two-year-old theater director and technician) met at a play rehearsal and ended up running a theater in Australia together: the natural venue for their wedding. Tony has Buddhist leanings and Joanna is agnostic and partially psychic. A friend who was a chaplain offered to be the celebrant.

Michael (a twenty-eight-year-old composer and violinist) and Mark (a thirty-four-year-old graphic designer) found that the nondogmatic spiritual views of the Unitarian church reflected how they felt: "We did not want a totally secular ceremony because spirituality is an important part of our lives."

Other couples felt free to follow their own beliefs. Lee (a thirty-three-year-old retailer) and Karen (a thirty-one-year-old student) designed a Pagan ceremony with elements of Buddhism and made it relevant to each of them. Apala (a twenty-five-year-old journalist) and Julian (a thirty-three-year-old publishing manager) searched long and hard for an open-air ceremony that reflected both her lapsed Catholic belief in God and angels and his passionate agnosticism. In the end they settled for a civil service followed by a ceremony conducted by a minister with "the imagination to share a God for all people."

One couple with a varied spiritual background faced a similar situation. Norman (a twenty-nine-year-old registered nurse) was raised a Christian but had pagan leanings, while Tymythy (a thirty-four-year-old hairstylist) had a racial background that included Jewish and Cherokee. His family was Quaker; he was baptized a Methodist, raised as a Jehovah's Witness, and at the time of the wedding was a practicing pagan. Thus it made sense for the couple to choose a pagan ritual.

Christianity as opposed to "churchianity." Robert and Miranda (a twenty-five-year-old writer and healer) felt that Christianity did have much to offer for them. They discovered, however, that the minister of the church they wanted to marry in (which was at the bottom of Robert's grandmother's garden) insisted they live in the parish for six months instead of what was in fact five months and three weeks before the date they had chosen! In the end, this ridiculous red tape led them to drop the church wedding in favor of a civil marriage followed by a ceremony in the garden.

Karen (a thirty-two-year-old physician) and Jean (a thirty-five-year-old church administrator) wanted to celebrate their union in a special and spiritual way. Both Christians, they were fortunate in that their pastor was prepared to write a ceremony based on the Christian wedding ceremony but that included positive affirmation of same-sex commitment.

A desire for simplicity. At its heart, a marriage is about two people committing themselves to each other for life. That is all. It is a big deal, but it's also a remarkably profound, intimate, and simple act, and it is quite understandable that you may not want to clutter it up with traditional trappings. As one couple said:

> We felt that church weddings seem to detract from the couple marrying. It's mainly for social acceptance and respectability, and to please family, relatives, and friends whom you never see at any other time. And they are so expensive!

Mixed marriages. It is becoming more and more common for couples from different countries, cultures, religions, and ethnic backgrounds to want to marry. Some religions are extremely strict and will not allow this; others are more flexible. The best way of combining the two is to pull elements of each together in a new unique ceremony, with two celebrants—one from each side—to officiate.

Family problems. If you have what sociologists today call a "blended" family, chances are not everyone will get along. Even without a proliferation of ex-wives, stepfathers, or half-siblings, weddings do tend to bring together parts of the family that are sometimes best separated. People are usually able to bury their differences for the sake of the couple marrying, although even in the most placid of families the run-up to a wedding can be traumatic and full of heated arguments. If your families cannot be safely gathered together, you might want to escape to a palm-fringed beach or have a quickie wedding in Las Vegas while on vacation. As Neil Hamilton (a transport manager) and Patricia Tierney (a thirty-five-year-old charity worker) said: "We decided to get married in Sarajevo because there's something special about the place, and because it's the only place our families couldn't come, and we wanted a quiet wedding." (*Daily Telegraph*, August 26, 1994)

If you come from a home with a different set-up from the traditional (though no longer common) nuclear family, you may also find the established wording of a traditional ceremony abrasive and inappropriate.

Second marriages. If either of you is marrying for the second or third time around, you will of course want to do it differently. A church wedding may not be possible (it is usually up to the discretion of the minister) and you would be forgiven for not wanting to repeat the exact vows you spoke years before with someone else. A wedding in the Seychelles islands was an ideal choice for one couple I interviewed. As Nicola (a thirty-one-year-old dentist) said:

> Pascal was divorced and neither of us are regular churchgoers so it didn't seem important to have the church sanctify our union. We fixed the date and time in consultation with an astrologer who studied our natal charts. In fact, at the wedding, a double rainbow appeared in the sky behind us.

They obviously made the right choice!

Practical considerations. Space, time, money . . . if you haven't got the luxury of an abundance of all three you will probably need to depart from the traditional formula. A white wedding "with all the trimmings" can cost thousands of dollars. So can a nontraditional wedding, of course, but with fewer conventions to meet, you will find the cost drops dramatically. Weddings combined with honeymoons are examples, as are weddings in your garden at home, weddings abroad, and simple, moving weddings with a few friends. Margaret (a twenty-five-year-old mental health care manager) and Colin (a twenty-four-year-old accountant), explained:

> We are atheists and our wedding was arranged on impulse, a decision made when we knew that our families would be spending Easter with us. We also had a very limited income at the time and had just had a baby—really we wanted the minimum of fuss.

Gay and lesbian couple. Gay couples cannot legally marry in most countries. Most organized religions publicly reject the practice of homosexuality. On top of these issues, all the above reasons apply to gay and lesbian couples as well. Martin (a twenty-eight-year-old sexual health educator) and Roy (a twenty-seven-year-old computer programmer) explained that one of them was a Spiritualist and the other a lapsed Catholic. They wanted a commitment ceremony that came from them, that reflected who they were, and that made a statement to friends and family. Another couple, Philip (a thirty-four-year-old local government official) and Steve (a twenty-eight-year-old chef), said they were both spiritual, although Philip was basically agnostic, while Steve was originally from a Baptist background but had stopped going to church due to what he saw as hypocrisy. They wanted their ceremony to bear as little resemblance to a heterosexual wedding as possible, to make their own statement, and to keep the seriousness of the occasion paramount.

Patrick (a twenty-seven-year-old corporate banker) and Don (a thirty-year-old studying for a Ph.D. in English literature) wanted to craft a unique ceremony that focused on the blessing of their union by friends, family, and community rather than invoking traditional authorities to "sanction" a union they had already established and to which they felt committed.

Renewing your vows. Couples are increasingly choosing to renew their vows, perhaps on a significant anniversary. This is a chance to have a public affirmation of your relationship and the values by which you have been living. Author Barbara Taylor Bradford renewed her vows during a second honeymoon in Antigua.

Although you may prefer not to replicate too many of the details of your original wedding, you might decide to follow the format of one of the ceremonies described in this book, adapting and altering it as appropriate. The officiant will offer help and advice, but keep it simple and warm.

Of course, in practice what drives couples to create their own alternative wedding is a combination of all of these reasons. For couples who think carefully about the kind of wedding they want, it seems to become increasingly impossible to opt for the traditional format, unless of course they are committed to a certain faith. Christine (a forty-two-year-old writer and relationships psychologist) and Mark (a thirty-five-year-old educational publisher) chose their wedding for several reasons:

> We wanted a ceremony that truly reflected who we were, and it was therefore largely designed and determined by us and to our criteria. We wanted a ritual that marked a rite of passage, and could not find one that reflected our beliefs honestly. We wanted a ceremony that fully involved everyone there in a very practical way.

Making the decision not to have a traditional church wedding does not automatically mean that the preparations running up to the day and dealings with your families will run completely smoothly. In some ways there are more initial difficulties to be overcome. However, with careful planning and a firm over-arching belief in the kind of wedding you both want, you may feel surprisingly free. Untrammelled by convention, you can simply get on with organizing the kind of day you want. Deciding to branch out and do your own thing can be a scary and isolating experience. It can also be incredibly liberating and exciting. This book will help you plan a stylish, original, and imaginative wedding, no matter what your beliefs.

I'd like to close this chapter with a caveat. Don't let your wedding day detract from your marriage. One is a celebration of the other. Your wedding day is undeniably an amazingly special one, but it is not the be-all and end-all, so do not focus all your energies just on this one day. In fact your wedding day is the beginning, just one of thousands of days you will hopefully be together. Start your married life together as you mean to go on: making decisions and choices as a couple.

ALTERNATIVE PROPOSALS

Before we move on to weddings themselves, you might like to consider different ways of asking for your partner's "hand in marriage." Even in these days of sexual equality, it is still fairly unusual for the woman to propose, but why wait for a leap year? Consider the women from the Trobriand Islands of Papua New Guinea, who approach their desired mate and bite him! For couples who have been together for years, there may not even be a need for one to propose to the other: you may have a mutual understanding that you want to spend your lives together and the wedding day becomes a practical, rather than a romantic decision.

Traditionally proposals are made over dinner or while on vacation, at Christmas, on Valentine's Day, or on birthdays. I know people who live on tenterhooks from special occasion to special occasion, wondering when The Question might be popped, or waiting anxiously for the most "romantic" moment to propose. What could be less spontaneous? If you want to avoid the clichés, choose a moment when your partner is least expecting it: in the bath, in the middle of an argument, in the fast lane of a motorway? Or send a surprise bunch of flowers with a note, leave a proposal on their pillow for them to find if you are away on business, or get a DJ to read it out on the radio. If you like grand, theatrical gestures, you could organize a fire-writing display to light up "Will you marry me?" in fireworks or post your proposal on a billboard on your partner's way home from work. You could even get an airplane to trail a message through the sky (contact your local general aviation airfield, who will let you know if it is something they can arrange).

The most unusual words used for a proposal that I came across were from a young man who, after years of pressure to get engaged, said to his girlfriend: "Well, shall we inform your parents of the imminent change in our cohabitational status then?" These were not words from the heart, and the wedding was cancelled two weeks before it was due to take place.

If what you want is a wedding from the heart, read on.

MARRIAGE PRAYER

During the time that you are engaged, try not to forget what you are doing and why you are doing it. Marriage is one of the deepest rites of passages we experience and offers feelings we must hold on to.

You might like to recite the following prayer—written by Robert and Miranda Holden—each day or each week leading up to your wedding, in order to prepare yourselves mentally for the life-enhancing event ahead:

> Oh Divine Creator of all this Wonder,
> We stand before you with our hearts and minds
> open and ready to receive Your Divine

*Inspiration, Clarity, and Truth in order
to create a beautiful, joyful, and
inspiring ceremony for our marriage.*

*We devote our union to You and thank You
infinitely for bringing us together.
May our marriage and all of our wedding
plans be blessed and inspired by You,
so that we can get closer to You in
order to unfold into our Highest
Purpose on Earth.*

*May this unfolding bring love and joy
to all those we meet, and may we have the
privilege of acting as channels
through which Your Divine Light may
enter the world.
So be it.*

2

Marriage and the Law

Marriage is a binding together of a man and
woman to live in an indivisible union.

Emperor Justinian

PLANNING a wedding is romantic and exciting: the air is charged
with promises made, and more to be made; you are the toast of your friends
and relatives; you are making plans for your life together. It can also be a
manically busy time, depending on the scale of the wedding you are
planning, the time you have, and the extent to which you are having to
cope with relatives who may disagree with the type of wedding you have
chosen. It is easy to forget at such a time one very important aspect of
marriage—its status as a legal agreement. Indeed, if you are intending to
have a nonchurch wedding, or want to know what your options for a civil
wedding are, you need to be crystal clear on where you stand. Of course,
you may decide not to have a legally recognized wedding at all.

Marriage has been variously described as a civil contract, a status, and
an institution. It has been around for thousands of years, and what to us is
a traditional Christian wedding is, in fact, relatively new. Originally
invented to promote the stability of society and for the protection of
women and children, marriage has far-reaching effects on both family and
social relationships, and carries with it rights and obligations: to children,
property, and to each other.

In the United States the laws affecting married couples vary from state
to state, so you'll need to check for yourself if you have any specific
questions not covered in this chapter, particularly regarding recent changes
in the law. Either ask the official in charge of granting licenses, who should

15

have some printed information covering the law, or failing that, try a law library (the county or city clerk will tell you where to find one).

However, there are some general guidelines that every state more or less conforms to, although the wording of the laws may vary slightly.

Circumstances whereby you *cannot* legally marry are as follows:

- If your partner is a close relative "within the fourth or fifth degree of relationship;" this includes half or whole blood and can include step-relations or in-laws, and even those related by adoption; it is sometimes possible for first cousins to marry if they are over a certain (reproductive) age, or if one is sterile; Native Americans and Jewish people are an exception to this: they are permitted by their own laws to marry close relatives
- If force or fraud has occurred
- If one or both partners are under the influence of alcohol or drugs
- Where a previous marriage has not ended in either death or divorce (several states have provisions for cases where the partner has been missing for a period of time, usually five to seven years) remember that some religions do not recognize second marriages, although happily this is becoming less common
- Where one or both partners are under age (the limit differs from state to state, from as young as fourteen to as old as twenty-one)
- Where one partner is "mentally incompetent," (for reasons of mental illness or retardation is unable to make responsible decisions concerning their person or property)
- If one partner is physically unable to consummate the marriage, unless the other is aware of the fact before the wedding
- If one partner has a transmissible disease such as AIDS, leprosy, "or other loathsome disease" that was concealed from the other person
- Where one partner has a felony conviction, has been a prostitute, or has been "notoriously licentious" and has concealed the fact from the intended spouse
- In the case of a woman being pregnant, without her partner's knowledge, with the child of another man; or if a man fathers a child by another woman within ten months of the marriage; these instances would give a spouse grounds for annulment

SAME-SEX MARRIAGES

Gay and lesbian marriages are denied legal status in almost all countries of the world. Despite the seeming immutablitiy of this fact, however, the question of legally sanctioned same-sex unions has been hotly debated in recent years both in the United States and abroad. Although the full results of the debate are yet to be determined, the opening of a dialogue on the topic has itself initiated some remarkable changes. In Denmark, Norway, Sweden, and Iceland, "registered partnerships" are legally accepted, but at least one partner must be a citizen and resident of the country to marry there, and such partnerships are not recognized in other countries. The Hungarian Parliament voted in May 1996 to begin recognizing same-sex common law marriages. In addition, the Netherlands is expected to pass legislation legalizing gay marriage sometime in 1997.

The issue earned a place in the U.S. spotlight because of a court case in Hawaii, where in 1993 the state supreme court ruled on the state's ban against issuing marriage licenses to same-sex couples. The case was sent back to a lower court because the supreme court felt the ban violated the state constitution. Back in the lower court, it fell to the state to prove a "compelling interest" in banning same-sex marriages.

In response to the possibility of legalized same-sex unions in Hawaii, the Defense of Marriage Act was introduced in the U.S. House of Representatives. The bill, which passed the House in July 1996, denies federal benefits to same-sex couples and allows each state to decide whether it would recognize same-sex marriages performed in other states. In September 1996, the bill was passed in the Senate and signed by President Clinton. Although the act does not criminalize these marriages and even reserves a state's right to recognize such unions if it sees fit, several states have already passed legislation banning recognition of same-sex marriages.

Meanwhile, in December 1996, Hawaiian circuit court judge Kevin Chang ruled that the state failed to show a compelling reason for discriminating against same-sex marriages and ordered the state to start issuing marriage licenses to same-sex couples. Although he immediately granted a stay on his decision pending another appeal to the state supreme court, many remain hopeful that the decision will stand, making Hawaii the first state in which gay and lesbian couples could legally marry.

The implications these events hold for the future legal status of gay and lesbian unions is the subject of endless debate. Despite these legal turmoils, however, more and more gay and lesbian couples are holding public affirmation and commitment ceremonies—several of which are included as examples in this book. They may not be legal, but they are certainly meaningful and important for the couples, their families, and friends.

Many couples have found that there *are* some legal steps they can take to protect themselves and each other. Although these do not affect the couple's marital status, they can provide the feeling that the couple is bound to each other by ties other than emotional ones. Some hyphenate their names. Other couples go further: Jean and Karen, for example, made wills, gave each other power of attorney, completed medical advance directives (giving each other the legal right to make medical decisions in the event of the other's incapacity), and they opened joint checking and savings accounts. Others include each other in their wills. Todd and Michael signed off on their house mortgage one month before their ceremony. Says Todd, "Legally, that bound us together far more than our ceremony. The wedding was an expression of our love to our loved ones and community, based on love not legality."

COMMON LAW MARRIAGE

Fourteen states recognize common law marriages, in which a couple lives together and represents themselves to those around them as husband and wife; twelve others have passed laws giving a cut-off date past which no new common law marriage will be recognized. The remaining states do not recognize them, unless the couple has moved from a state that did recognize the marriage at the time of the declaration.

LEGAL REQUIREMENTS

Following are some basic conditions required of all legal marriages:

- No matter what kind of religious or nonreligious ceremony you choose, you will need to obtain a license from the official connected with the location where you decide to get married. Take along a copy of your birth certificate and proof of identification and residence. Fees and waiting periods for licenses vary from state to state. The license will be valid anywhere from thirty days to one year, depending on the state. If you over-run the time limit without marrying, you will need to reapply.

- If you are between the ages of sixteen and eighteen you will need the consent of one or both parents or a guardian, and this person may need to accompany you when you apply for the license. Some states may allow an under age girl to marry, usually if she is pregnant.
- Some states require a blood test for venereal disease and AIDS, a proof of rubella vaccine (for women), and a test for sickle cell anemia in certain high-risk groups. Results of the blood tests are given to the couple to ensure each is aware of the other's condition: the state will not intervene in the case of positive results.
- After the ceremony (required by most but not all states) the license and a certificate are signed by the couple, the official, and the witnesses. The couple keep the certificate and the license is returned to the place of issue in order that the marriage can be properly recorded.
- In the United States you may marry wherever you choose, as long as the person officiating agrees. Only one state, Hawaii, specifically states that the couple and the official must all be in the same place at the same time for the ceremony.
- Fifteen states specify that there must be witnesses, usually two, but there generally are two people who sign the license and certificate as official witnesses in all states.

THE CEREMONY

There is no set legal format for a wedding ceremony, and it may vary according to your religious beliefs, and whether it is small or large, formal or informal. You are free to write your own vows or opt to go with the standard wording provided by your religious or civil official. In this book you will find many alternative ceremonies that I hope will provide an inspirational starting point for your own ceremony.

A civil ceremony will be conducted by a civil official, and depending on the state, he could be anything from a Justice of the U.S. Supreme Court to a local notary public—as long as they are licensed by the state to perform marriage ceremonies. A religious ceremony is not required by law, but if you do choose one you will find that at least one of you will probably be expected to be a member of the faith of the minister performing the service. Some have a written ceremony to follow; others allow you to write your own. Many states recognize ceremonies performed in accordance with the beliefs of Indian tribes or nations, those of Jewish or Islamic faith, the Quakers, or Baha'is. It is simply a matter of locating a member of the organization or religious tradition who is authorized to perform marriage ceremonies. Remember that, regardless of the religious requirements, a civil license must still be obtained and a record of the marriage filed. If you are uncertain about the legality of the ceremony you are planning, consult the civil official from whom you obtain your marriage license.

GETTING MARRIED ABROAD

In most countries marriages must be registered separately with the civil authorities. The main thing to remember is that the law of the country prevails. Two witnesses are usually required plus the "marriage officer." The marriage needs to be registered, and you should obtain copies of the documentation (as well as translations into English). On board a ship the marriage can be performed by a chaplain or ranking members of the crew (be sure to ask who will be available when making your plans). If you marry abroad your wedding will not be registered at home, but it will be legally recognized. You may lodge a copy of your certificate and any accompanying translations with the county clerk or records clerk, who could provide copies if they are needed.

Laws vary from country to country, but you will probably need to check whether you should take:

- birth certificates (plus copies)
- letters stating you are employed (plus copies)
- a decree nisi (documentition of divorce), if applicable
- proof of single status
- passport photos
- translations of the above documents
- a certificate of "nonimpediment"

Marriage and the Law

When you are there you may need to:

- place a notice in a local newspaper asking for declarations of any just impediment
- post banns (an official announcement) for a required number of days
- find two witnesses (although you could just pluck them from the street)
- hire a translator
- have a blood test (it is often possible to have these on the morning of your wedding)
- have a chest X-ray
- spend a few days in the country before marrying

The time you will have to spend there before you can marry varies from country to country. Curiously enough, European countries can be the most problematic for nonindigenous couples wishing to marry. In Italy, for example, you must stay in the country for six weeks. In the Caribbean they vary from island to island. Barbados, for example, requires one day's residence, St. Lucia two days' residence plus three days' paperwork. Antigua, Thailand, Jamaica, St. Kitts, St. Vincent, and the British Virgin Islands all require three days' residence. For Bali you will have to be resident for seven days, plus a day in Jakarta to deal with the paperwork. Don't forget that there will be a fee, which again differs from country to country.

If you want to be clear about what the requirements are for the country you have chosen, phone the relevant foreign consulate (a local government official may be able to help you locate the appropriate office), stating your intention to marry in their country. They will advise you of the correct procedures. Alternatively, if you are going on a wedding/honeymoon package, the tour company will have all the answers and will usually fix all the legal niceties for you.

Remember, you may be dealing with a language you don't understand and may have trouble getting through the red tape. It could take longer to organize than you think.

CHANGING YOUR NAME

Traditionally women took on their husband's last name upon marriage. This practice, although not legally enforced, is no longer automatic and some states have passed laws that allow women to retain their previous name.

If you do decide to change your name, you will need to send a copy of your marriage certificate to any relevant official bodies in order to ask them to change their records and issue you with new documents. Bear in mind the following:

- car registration
- driving license
- passport
- auto organization
- insurance policies
- pension plans
- building society
- bank for check book and cards
- credit card companies
- accounts department at work

If you do not have a marriage certificate, an attorney can arrange for your names to be changed legally and will issue a certificate accordingly. Some people, on changing their name, send out a card to friends and business associates announcing the fact.

3

The Important Day

ALTHOUGH you have decided you do not want a traditional white wedding, it is important for you and your guests to take the wedding seriously. You need to "feel married" afterward. For this reason there are ritualistic, social, and cultural elements you might want to include in order to add gravity to the proceedings. You may want to select elements from the following list:

- a sacred, beautiful, or unusual setting
- a celebrant
- formal invitations
- special clothes for the bride, groom, and guests
- a best man, bridesmaids, or supporters
- arrival and "handing over" from one family to another
- a circular format
- flowers
- music
- readings
- prayers
- vows
- exchange of rings
- a receiving line
- a postwedding meal
- cake

- speeches
- singing and dancing
- confetti and "going away"
- wedding gifts
- special touches
- a postwedding trip

It is not the intention of this book to prescribe what you should or should not do, nor how far ahead of the "big day" each element should be booked, although there is a checklist at the back of this book, so you can make sure you have all the elements you want to include covered. It is *your* wedding and can, therefore, be as simple or elaborate as you wish. One word of warning, however. If you do want to include several of these elements and time is short, you will probably need help from friends or parents. Don't hold back from asking them—you will find that people will be glad to help as long as they know what you want. Alternatively, you could contact a consultant to deal with the bookings, the preparation, and planning, while you concentrate on each other.

The first thing you need to decide is what style of wedding you want, the location, and a few alternative dates. If astrology is important to you then you may want to consult an astrologer to determine the most favorable day and time—be aware, though, that it might not turn out to be very convenient! This chapter will help you make your choices, get you thinking, and start you on the journey towards creating your wedding. Then we will move on to the ceremony itself.

A SACRED, BEAUTIFUL, OR UNUSUAL SETTING

The location of your wedding is probably the single most important thing you will need to decide. It will affect all your other plans and may influence what you wear, the style of your invitations, what you and your guests eat and drink and the entire atmosphere of your wedding. Decide first what tone you want to set: intimate, exotic, fun, religious, formal, theatrical, or social.

If you do not already have a firm idea of location in mind, here are some options for you to consider:

Country

- Home.
- Anywhere else! The list is as long as there are countries and cities: a romantic city like Florence or Vienna, a tropical island, or a boat on the Nile. See chapter seven for more suggestions.

Venue

- Civil building, such as a town hall.
- Synagogue, church, or other place of worship. Clearly this will depend on your religious leanings and background.
- Hotel. Most luxurious hotels produce brochures detailing wedding packages they offer.
- Stately home. Contact your local historical society or tourism board to find preserved estates or other historical buildings that might be available for bookings.
- Museum or art gallery. Such slightly off-beat venues provide fantastic opportunities for unusual settings and "theme" weddings. It's best to phone the venue in question to check availability.
- Theme park, zoo, botanical garden, ranch, or other vacation getaway. Although the Vatican recently issued a proclamation discouraging the practice, many weddings are held every year at places like Disneyland—complete with Cinderella ballgowns and coaches with footmen!
- Sporting venues.
- River boat or barge.
- Cruise liner. On board ship you will usually find an official who is authorized to conduct marriage services at sea.
- Outside. Whether in a park, on the beach, beside a river bank, on a mountain, in a forest glade, or under a gazebo in your own garden, open-air weddings are unusual and romantic. Add atmosphere with candles or fairy lights, fill bowls with rose petals and scented water. Drape tables with lengths of material, hang muslin on walls, decorate with ivy, wheat, fruit, and flowers; scatter herbs and spices on floors. If you are artistic you could even paint an evocative backdrop.
- Up in the air or under water. We're talking adventurous here: hot-air balloon, parachute, bungee, or helicopter. Remember, space is

limited and you will have to seek out an open-minded officiant or celebrant from one of the traditions described later in the book.

- Hospital. Nursing staff are usually happy to arrange bedside weddings, as long as the patient is not too ill. I did talk to one woman, Christine, who married her long-time partner, Jim, in the hospital where he was dying of cancer.

- Virtual reality. Yes, it is now happening in cyberspace: at least one U.S. company is pioneering virtual matrimony, which makes it possible to conduct your marriage anywhere without going anywhere, by means of electronic images transmitted through headsets. The bride and groom don identical "vision immersion headsets," through which they are assailed by visions of hearts, doves, and flowers while they are transported in a horse-drawn carriage to a castle in the sky. The computerized vision is simultaneously projected onto a video screen for the benefit of the rest of the wedding party. It is incredibly expensive, and I leave you to decide how meaningful it might be.

- On the Internet. Some priests make a speciality of marrying couples on the net—even those who have never met each other!

A CELEBRANT

A celebrant is the person who officiates at the wedding: for traditional weddings it would be a minister, priest, rabbi, and so on. Many couples feel it is appropriate to have their ceremony conducted by a "wise elder," who will often say something about the couple, about marriage, about religious or moral guiding principles (if relevant), and about sharing a future together. This lends gravity to the occasion and gives the wedding a wider meaning.

Depending on the type of wedding you choose, the choice of celebrant is very much up to you. If you want to marry in a particular church, the minister usually comes as part of the package (although many are often prepared to share the service with another ordained preacher who is a friend of the couple). It would be a very open-minded minister who would allow a rabbi or representative from another religious tradition to co-officiate the ceremony, but if you ask around, you may find one who is prepared to be flexible. Civil officials will take you through the procedure in advance and conduct the ceremony. Other disciplines, such as the Humanists or Druids, will give you the names of official celebrants who will conduct weddings in your area—but you may also choose a friend or relative, or conduct the wedding yourselves. Some, such as Quaker weddings, do not require a celebrant at all, and the couple effectively marry themselves. See Part II for more detailed information on the different alternative wedding ceremonies and how to go about organizing them.

FORMAL INVITATIONS

If you were having a traditional church wedding, you might feel limited by convention as to what you should print on the invitation. This can lead to agonizing problems for some couples, whether their parents are divorced and have remarried, they are marrying for the second time, or the groom's parents are footing the bill. Even the size of type and the shape of the invitation itself follow a standard format.

This, from *Emily Post on Second Weddings* (Elizabeth L. Post, HarperPerennial, 1991), is advice on putting the invitation into the envelope:

> The invitation, folded edge first, is put in the inner envelope with the printed side toward the flap. The cards are inserted in front of it, with the reception card next to the invitation and any smaller cards in front of that. The inner envelope, unsealed, is placed in the outer envelope with the flap away from you.

I suggest you ignore this (even if you understand what it means!) The joy of nontraditional weddings is that anything goes. Forget etiquette: from a phone call or a short, handwritten note, to a printed card, the wording is up to you—just choose whatever you are most comfortable with. The following elements may or may not be included:

- your names (either just first names or names and surnames)
- venue for the ceremony
- venue for the postceremony celebration, if separate

- date and time
- address for RSVP
- any travel/accommodation instructions or suggestions
- appropriate dress
- a poem or quotation
- your parents' or guardians' names (if they are paying for or hosting the wedding)
- your children's names

If you are artistic, why not design the invitations yourself and give the artwork to a local printer? Alternatively, there are companies who will design and print different stationery for you, with floral designs, gold, silver, or medieval lettering, ribbons to match your color scheme, or another motif which picks up the theme of your wedding (leaves and berries, for example, for an outdoor autumn wedding). Some do beautiful calligraphy and pressed flowers; some include sachets of confetti; others print invitations on balloons. Some will also design location maps for your guests. The invitations to a fancy dress wedding I once attended were illustrated with a child's drawing of the couple.

On the front of your invitation you could have a pencil sketch or photograph of your wedding location, a decoupage illustration, or a photograph of yourselves. You could also print a few words:

And we shall become one
to share all the days
of our lives . . .

If there is anything better than
to be loved, it is loving.

Today is the first day
of our life together.

We have something very special
we want to share with you.

Today we begin sharing
our life . . .
. . . our love.

The Important Day

Two lives, two hearts
joined together in friendship
united together in love

We will share our tomorrows
and all that they hold.

Or choose a quote from an anthology on love, such as Eileen Campbell's *A Lively Flame* (HarperCollins, 1992).

Some couples prefer to give a special, formal touch to their invitations. For others, simple handwritten invitations chime in with the informal, natural style of their wedding. Again, it is entirely up to you, but it is a good idea to match the feel of the invitations with the feel of the wedding. Here are some examples of invitations used by couples I interviewed.

Alison Hollis and Geoff Wakefield
together with their children
request the honor of your presence at
their wedding
on
Friday, May 5th
at 3 o'clock
in the garden of Abbotsbrook Hotel

Sarah and Katy
invite you to celebrate with us our
Ceremony of Love and Commitment
followed by lunch
on
Sunday, July 18th
4 p.m.
at 67 Manor Road

Alternative Weddings

⚘

David and Robert
request the honor of your presence
the weekend of the summer solstice
and invite you to share in their
lifelong love and commitment
to each other in a
Ceremony of Affirmation
Saturday, the 21st of June, 1996
at six o'clock
at the home of Tim Garth
1183 Yardley Street
Reception immediately following

If you are holding a party after your wedding—let's say you married abroad and none of your friends attended the wedding, or you are marrying for a second time—but don't want people to feel they need to bring gifts, simply send party invitations without mentioning your marriage. If guests then RSVP to a friend, the friend can explain your wishes.

No matter how informal your wedding, guests like to have service sheets or a ceremony outline. For alternative weddings, it can be helpful to be able to hand out a copy of the ceremony, or at the very least a guide to the proceedings. Many couples I spoke to said this was a good way of introducing their guests (most of whom had never been to an alternative wedding before) to the kind of wedding they had chosen. It also helps things run more smoothly if any audience participation is required.

SPECIAL CLOTHES FOR THE BRIDE, GROOM, AND GUESTS

Traditionally, of course, the groom wears morning dress and the bride wears white. The white wedding dress was largely a product of the nineteenth century, a time when people were obsessed with virginity and purity. Silk, taffeta, chiffon, lace, satin . . . most brides do want to wear something special, although rampant frills and ruffles are no longer quite the thing. Even traditional brides are now wearing understated, simple dresses.

Remember, however, if you don't wear something that stands out, it might be difficult to pick yourself out in the photos—you definitely don't want to look like just another guest!

British television personality Muriel Gray, who married Hamish Barbour on a beach in the Hebrides, wore a daring (for the weather) off-the-shoulder dress made of tartan, while Hamish wore a kilt. "It's the only day in your life you're entitled to go over the top," she says. This advice was endorsed by Paula Yates, whose beautiful, scarlet, duchess satin wedding dress and veil certainly looked dramatic for her (second) wedding to Bob Geldof. But beware the excesses of Brigitte Nielsen when she married Sylvester Stallone: her dress arrived in its own limousine and had to be escorted by three policemen into the mansion where the wedding was held. Or Masako Owada, who, on her wedding to Crown Prince Naruhito of Japan, had to wear court robes weighing thirty pounds. And, of course, we all heard about *Baywatch* babe Pamela Anderson and her white bikini wedding.

There are plenty of folk sayings about The Dress: who sees it, the significance of the number of buttons, how soon before the wedding it should be finished, the fortunes of the seamstress who sews the dress . . . most of which are irrelevant to this book, which seeks to leave tradition behind. Although tradition may have been abandoned by many of the couples I interviewed, I discovered superstition definitely had not. Even some of the most alternative brides still go for "something old, something new, something borrowed, something blue." Although fewer add "a silver sixpence in your shoe," the forgotten last line of the ditty, one gay man taped a penny to the sole of his bare foot.

Here is an old poem about the color or your wedding dress that shows just how much times have changed:

> Married in white, you have chosen right
> Married in black, you will wish yourself back
> Married in red, you will wish yourself dead
> Married in green, ashamed to be seen
> Married in grey, you will go far away
> Married in blue, love ever true
> Married in pearl, you will live in a whirl
> Married in yellow, ashamed of your fellow

Alternative Weddings

Married in pink, of you he'll aye think.

It's your day, so make the most of your opportunity to do something wild and different. At a church wedding I attended once, the bride (who probably hadn't been in a church for years) turned up in a gorgeous bright pink dress and veil—the entire congregation gasped with delight.

Veils were originally used to protect the bride from the glances of jealous suitors. Today it's not essential, even in church weddings, but they can look rather glamorous. If you do decide to wear one you might want to choose an unusual color and pile it up on top of your head, twist it round, or pin it up.

Although it is true that anything goes at alternative weddings, choose something that suits your looks, your personality, and the wedding. Here is a list of ideas for you to draw inspiration from:

- Dresses of silk, chiffon, lace, or taffeta in any color: cream, purple, red, green, and blue were particularly popular with the nontraditional brides I spoke to; one woman dressed her bridesmaids in black, and some grooms chose to match their bride's dress, with patterned vests, cravats, or even white silk suits
- Traditional dress from your or your partner's country or religious tradition, or to match the location or style of your wedding: Indian sari, Nehru suit, tribal robes, Chairman Mao jacket, oriental dress, baggy silk trousers, tie-die costumes with rich headdresses; gay couples often wear matching jewelry
- Authentic clothing worn at the time your chosen wedding originated: Elizabethan costume, Viking dress, Russian-style garments, plain seventeenth-century puritan clothing
- Fancy dress: '20s, '50s, or '60s—choose any decade this century—or go medieval, Victorian, or rock 'n' roll; get your guests to dress up too, and have a masked ball afterwards!
- Evening dress: ball gown and black tie
- Casual: T-shirts and jeans
- Beachwear

Get a dress-making friend to run something up for you, or try second-hand shops. You might even want to dye your mother's old wedding dress, or alter it to a more up-to-date style to suit you. If you are having a dress made, have the final fitting just before the wedding. And don't forget sexy underwear and garters, which I discovered were de rigueur with alternative brides!

Make sure your guests know what they are expected to wear, so they don't feel awkward in traditional hat and morning dress. Many alternative couples ask their guests to dress "comfortably." If you are going to be dancing, tramping through woods, or sitting down at a picnic afterwards, plan your clothes appropriately. And remember, if your wedding is going to be outside, make sure you take umbrellas and warm wraps just in case. For foreign weddings, even if you are going to an exotic island, do check in an atlas for temperature and rainfall in the month of your wedding. Some couples get caught out!

Be careful not to let The Dress ruin the run-up to the wedding, as it can do for many a traditional bride. Yes, you want to look special, but every bride looks beautiful on her wedding day, no matter what she is wearing. As Nicola said, "It truly would have meant the same to me even if I'd been wearing a cloth sack."

A BEST MAN, BRIDESMAIDS, OR SUPPORTERS

If you have chosen to have an alternative wedding, it is quite likely that you will be organizing it yourselves and may well need some extra support. The tradition for having supporters goes way back to pre-Christian times and appears in many weddings of different religions. In India, for example, brides go through a purification ritual before their wedding, where they are bathed and anointed with different oils by their women friends and relatives. In Czechoslovakia, a married couple, selected by the bride and groom, help organize the day and are responsible for leading the songs, cheering and the final placing of the "apron of marriage" on the new wife as she departs with her husband.

Originally the best man was a friend of the bridegroom who helped him kidnap the bride. Although today you do not legally require a best man or bridesmaids, many couples do choose to enlist assistance. As well as helping in the run-up to the wedding, it gives a sense of support and groundedness during the ceremony itself to know that you have your closest friends on hand involved in your wedding and witnessing your vows.

Other options are to have a "best person" each, perhaps a male for the bride and a female for the groom, who can take you to the wedding and give a reading or a speech. Or you could do as the Druids do and nominate five people to participate in the ceremony. Young children, favoured by traditional brides, can add to the fun and lend a family feel to the occasion, but they do need supervision and can detract from the solemnity of the ceremony by running amok. The most unusual choice of best man I have come across was millionaire advertising man Eric Forbes, who chose his dog Bobo as best man. Apparently the terrier turned up at the ceremony dressed in a $700 Versace suit with two rings in a pocket!

ARRIVAL AND HANDING OVER FROM ONE FAMILY TO ANOTHER

The couples I spoke to were divided on this point. Of course, in traditional church weddings, the bride is conducted down the aisle by her father and symbolically handed over to her husband-to-be. The groom may not turn round until she arrives at his side.

If you have been living together for some time, you may feel that as you are already established as a couple, it is more appropriate for you to arrive together as equal partners. In some Catholic countries, the bride and groom meet outside the church and walk in together, followed by the rest of the congregation. In Jewish weddings, the entire wedding party processes down the aisle led by the rabbi, with the bride bringing up the rear. If you want to do this, you may find an open-minded minister who will agree. Or you could be escorted by a son, brother, mother, or close friend, who could embrace you or kiss your hand as they hand it to the groom.

It is also often acceptable to alter the wording from "who gives this woman to be married . . ." to "who presents this woman to be married," or "who represents the families in blessing this marriage?" And don't feel you have to keep your back turned—you could copy the Jewish custom where the groom watches his bride walk toward him.

On the other hand, some couples like the ritual significance of arriving separately from two different lives, two different families, each giving their blessing on the couple who become one new unit. One way of having the best of both worlds might be to process to your wedding separately, followed by your families, and meet your partner outside the wedding, join hands, and enter together.

A CIRCULAR FORMAT

No matter how alternative the ceremony, many women still want the feel of walking down an aisle to meet their future husband. If your father is involved, you may want to indulge his long-cherished wish to walk you down the aisle, even though you may be in a forest glade with seats arranged as if in pews. A circular format has ritual and spiritual significance, and certainly gives a wedding a different feel. It involves the guests more fully in the wedding and lends an intimate atmosphere. A circle will also allow you to be seen by everyone, but if you do have square seating, it is still possible to turn and face your guests during the ceremony, with the celebrant facing you or at one side. Alternatively, you and your partner can turn and face each other, rather than the celebrant, throughout the ceremony.

FLOWERS

No wedding, no matter how low-key, seems complete without flowers, which can add glory and charm to the simplest ceremony. Whether you carry a simple lily or have an extravagant display, flowers do lend beauty and freshness to wedding celebrations. Arranging them beforehand can be a fun activity for friends and family to share, especially if you have arranged the rest of the wedding yourself. You might want to consider including berries, herbs, fruit, and wheatsheafs, for a natural, country feel. Tie your bouquet with raffia rather than ribbon: I always think a pretty, hand-tied bunch can be much nicer than a stiff, formal bouquet. If your budget is limited, you can achieve wonderful effects with small table arrangements in terracotta pots with candles.

The Victorians accorded special significance to flowers, which provided a useful code for lovers to pass each other coy messages. These are of limited relevance today, but, if you really want to know that a carnation means true love and a cornflower hope, there are plenty of books to guide you. My advice is to choose flowers for their color, shape, and price. For a striking display, go for exotic blooms like orchids and the orange and purple Bird of Paradise, or giant daisies in buttonholes and on the cake can be fun. One couple asked each guest to bring a sunflower, which made for a stunning, summery effect. Contact local hospitals and charities, who may be delighted to have your flowers after the wedding.

MUSIC

Music is usually an integral part of any wedding ceremony: Shakespeare got it right when he suggested that it is the food of love. It adds mood and atmosphere and can echo the words or sense of the ceremony. It can also convey feelings that words alone cannot. Many couples choose reflective, quiet music before the ceremony, with an uplifting tune as the bride (and groom) arrive, romantic love songs during the wedding if there is a lull in the proceedings, followed by rousing, triumphant music when it is over. You can also use background music to accompany the spoken sections of your wedding.

If some of your guests are religious or used to traditional weddings, you might want to help them feel comfortable with the more familiar wedding tunes and hymns—but don't choose your music just to suit your guests. There is nothing to stop you choosing jazz, folk, pop, country, songs from films or musicals, love songs, harp, string quartet, swing, rock, reggae, steel band, sax and piano duo, trumpet fanfare, or a Scottish piper. The choice will depend on your taste and the setting and, sometimes, the wishes of the celebrant—particularly if you are marrying in a church. But why limit yourself to music for your background sounds? For outdoor weddings you could play birdsong tapes or recordings of crashing waves, or simply hang chimes to sing in the wind.

Your favorite artists have probably recorded several love songs, but here is a selection to get you going:

Uplifting or Rousing Music
Instrumental:

The Important Day

"Trumpet Tune": Charpentier
Water Music: Handel
"Arrival of the Queen of Sheba": Handel
Trumpet Tune and Air in D: Purcell
"Bridal Chorus" (*Lohengrin*): Wagner
Music for the Royal Fireworks: Handel
Trumpet Voluntary: Jeremiah Clarke
March Triomphale: John Field
"Wedding March" (*A Midsummer Night's Dream*): Mendelssohn
Processional (*The Sound of Music*): Richard Rodgers
"Pomp and Circumstance": Elgar

Hymns:
"Amazing Grace"
"Jerusalem"
"Now Thank We All Our God"
"A Safe Stronghold"
"Love Divine"
"Praise to the Holiest"
"Come Down, O Love Divine"
"Glorious Things of Thee Are Spoken"

Songs:
"Say You'll Be Mine": Christopher Cross
"Tell Me that You Love Me": Eric Clapton
"Space Age Love Song": Flock of Seagulls
"Stepping Out": Joe Jackson
"Perfect": Fairground Attraction
"Stand by Your Man": Tammy Wynette
"Never Gonna Give You Up": Rick Astley
"Love You": Syd Barrett
"Wouldn't It Be Nice": Beach Boys

Quiet or Romantic Music

Pieces:
"Jesu Joy of Man's Desiring": Bach

"Sheep May Safely Graze": Bach
Various choral preludes: Bach
Pathetique Sonata (slow mvt): Beethoven
Moonlight Sonata (slow mvt): Beethoven
Pastoral Symphony (*Messiah*): Handel
"Every Valley" (*Messiah*): Handel
Nimrod (*Enigma Variations*): Elgar
"Chanson de Matin/Nuit": Elgar
"Salut d'Amour": Elgar
Toccata in C: Pachelbel
"Ave Maria": Bach/Gounod
Water Music: Handel
"Ave Venum Corpus": Mozart
Pavane: Ravel
Allegro from Sonata in F: Handel
Polonaise in A Major: Chopin
Gymnopedie: Erik Satie
"Summertime": Gershwin
New World Symphony (slow mvt): Dvorak
Serenade: Schubert
Selections from *Rosamunde*: Schubert
Cavatina (theme music from *The Deer Hunter*): Stanley Myers
"God Be in My Head": Walford Davies
"Annie's Song": John Denver

Songs:
"My Beloved Spake": Patrick Hadley
"Sound the Trumpet": Purcell
"Laudate Dominum": Mozart
"Beati Quorum Via": C. V. Stamford
"A Love Song": traditional/words by Ben Jonson
"Ode to Joy": Beethoven/words by Schiller
"A Nightingale Sang in Berkeley Square": Manning Sherwin
"Close to You": The Carpenters
"I Could Have Danced All Night": *My Fair Lady*
"You're My Best Friend": Queen
"Amazing Grace": Julie Collins

"You'll Never Walk Alone": various
"Everything I Do I Do for You": Bryan Adams
"Riverdance": Bill Whelan
"Caracena": Bill Whelan
"Have I Told You Lately that I Love You": Van Morrison
"Wonderful World": Sam Cooke
"First Time Ever I Saw Your Face": Roberta Flack
"Stand By Me": Ben E. King
"Hopelessly Devoted to You": Olivia Newton John
"Part of Me; Part of You": Glen Frey
"Nights in White Satin": Moody Blues
"Perfect Day": Lou Reed
"I Want You": Bob Dylan
"Wonderful Tonight": Eric Clapton
"You Do Something to Me": Cole Porter
"Night and Day": Cole Porter
"My Favorite Things": Julie Andrews
"John Riley": The Byrds
"Blue Eyes": The International Submarine Band
"Bury Me Deep in Love": The Triffids
"Love Is All Around": The Troggs
"One Moment in Time": Whitney Houston
"A Long and Lasting Love": Glenn Medeiros
"The Best of Times": *La Cage aux Folles*
"Moongirl": Barclay James Harvest
"I Get a Kick out of You": Gary Shearston
"Loving and Free": Kiki Dee
"Nightingales": Prefab Sprout
"Broken Arrow": Robbie Robertson
"All of My Life": Diana Ross
"My Love": Paul McCartney
"Someone Like You": Van Morrison
"True Companion": Mark Cohen

Psalms:
67 Let the peoples praise thee
130 Out of the deep

150 O praise God in his holiness

Joyful Exit Music:

"All You Need Is Love": The Beatles
"Eight Days a Week": The Beatles
"You're the Top": Cole Porter
"True Love": Cole Porter
Polovtsian Dance (*Prince Igor*): Borodin
"I Was Glad": Parry
"Toccata": Widor
"Grand March" (*Aida*): Verdi

READINGS

This is your opportunity to add another dimension to your wedding through literary, secular, or spiritual works. They can be joyful, contemplative, traditional, or unusual. If read by friends or relatives, it is a chance to involve people who are important to you in the ceremony. The words spoken during a wedding are sacred, part of your own rite of passage. To enhance the vows you are making and the words of the officiant, add favorite poems or spiritual readings—even a love letter or words on a card your partner once sent you. If you can't think of anything immediately, visit your local library and scour love poetry collections, wedding anthologies, or even dictionaries of quotations, which might jog your memory or lead you to a special piece. You could also make selections from different religious traditions. The *Talmud*, the *Koran*, the *Upanishads*, the *Bhagavad Gita*, *A Course in Miracles*, and many other sources too numerous to list here will all provide inspiration. For gay weddings, consult the recently published, *We Were Baptized, Too: Claiming God's Grace for Lesbians and Gays*, by Marilyn Alexander and James Preston.

Here's a suggested list of starting points (unfortunately, there is not scope in a book of this size to print these wonderful readings and poems in full):

The Important Day

Poems

"Two in the Campagna": Browning
"My true love hath my heart and I have his": Sir Philip Sidney
"Come live with me and be my love": Christopher Marlowe
"One word is too often profaned": Shelley
"You are a part of me": Frank Yerby
"It is for the union of you and me": Rabindranath Tagore
"How do I love thee? Let me count the ways": Elizabeth Barrett
    Browning
"Shall I compare thee to a summer's day?": Shakespeare (Sonnet)
"If music be the food of love": Shakespeare (*Twelfth Night*)
"Drink to me only with thine eyes": Ben Jonson
"She walks in beauty": Byron
"John Anderson my Jo": Robert Burns
"She walks in beauty": Edgar Allan Poe
"A dedication to my wife": T.S. Eliot
"Sudden Light": Christina Rossetti
"From pent-up, aching rivers": Walt Whitman
"Winter Love": Elizabeth Jennings
"September": Ted Hughes
"The Good Morrow": John Donne
"Dream of a common language": Adrienne Rich
"When you are old and grey": W.B. Yeats
"Love's Philosophy": Shelley
"Love": William Temple
"A Birthday": Christina Rossetti
"Now you will feel no rain": American Indian poem
"Your breast is enough": Pablo Neruda
"The Owl and the Pussycat": Edward Lear

Biblical Extracts

Love is patient and kind . . .1 Corinthians 13:4–8a
Little children, let us not love in word and speech but in deed and in
truth . . . 1 John 3:18–24
Behold, let us love one another . . . 1 John 4:7–12
The Beatitudes . . . Matthew 5:2–4

This I command you, to love one another . . . John 15:11–17
Extracts from the Song of Solomon

Passages from Books

There are various books in which you may find passages to quote, such as:
The Prophet—Kahlil Gibran
Return to Love—Marianne Williamson
In Tune with the Infinite—Ralph Waldo Trine
Healing the Wounds: The Promise of Ecofeminism—Judith Plant
Soul Mates—Thomas Moore
Journey of the Heart—John Welwood
The Art of Loving—Erich Fromm
The Psychology of Romantic Love—Robert A. Johnson

VOWS

Whether you are writing your own or not, regard the planning of the ceremony and the vows in particular as an integral part of your marriage, not simply your wedding day.

What you are saying on your wedding day is that you love your partner. What you are promising is that you will love them tomorrow—and forever. This is also a promise to grow together through the experiences life throws at you and the promise through which you both are offering each other the chance to become the people you were meant to be. As Daphne Rose Kingma says in *Weddings from the Heart* (Conari Press, 1991):

> Marriage is an invitation to transcend the human condition. For in stepping beyond the self-focus of wanting only to have our own needs met, in schooling ourselves in the experience of putting another human being and his or her needs in a position of equal value to our own, we touch the web of transcendence, the presence of the divine.

The act of creating your own ceremony is an intimate and exposing one. Rather than allowing the traditional, familiar biblical words to wash over you and your guests, you are in effect stepping forward in a much more revealing manner to air the very personal nature of your own relationship. This makes nontraditional weddings highly emotionally charged events. As Christine said:

> I cried throughout, Mark was smiling but moved, most of the women in the audience and many of the men were in tears. Most people in the circle hugged or held on to each other as we made our vows. Once the ceremony was over, there was a spontaneous rush from everyone to hug and kiss us both.

There are likely to be people attending your ceremony for whom a nonreligious wedding is new. If your words are sincere and reflect your own beliefs, you will find that everyone will respect your chosen style of wedding.

It is said that your vows will determine what your future life together will be like. I believe that what you say on the day will be what you get. And the more you think about and care about the vows, the better things will be. Many couples I spoke to wrote their own vows. Others adapted existing wording found in books. The basic format of wedding vows is as follows:

1. Declaration from both partners that they are willing to take the other in marriage.
2. Solemn promises from each partner to each other that they will love and care for each other, come what may.

You don't have to follow this format, but it does give a feel of being part of an ancient rite. In some Pagan weddings the couple take fifteen minutes apart to compose their own vows there and then. They either declare them out loud or say them silently. Think about what you want to convey. Why have you chosen marriage rather than cohabitation? What does it mean to your relationship? What do you want to tell your guests about the meaning of marriage? What do you regard as important in a life relationship? Note down separately the key words and phrases that, for you, sum up your partnership and your hopes for the future. For example:

- How you met and how your relationship developed
- Mutual love and support
- Fidelity

- Working through challenges together
- Accepting each other's reality rather than adoring a mythical perfection
- Playing an active part in the community
- Allowing each other the space to develop and grow
- Children
- Your hopes and desires for the future

If you are marrying for the second or third time, resist the temptation to refer to your first marriage as incomplete or inadequate. Look to the future and a fresh start.

In Part II you will find suggestions and examples of vows from a variety of alternative weddings.

EXCHANGE OF RINGS

Rings have been worn since the third millennium B.C. Perhaps more significant than any other piece of jewelry, they have always represented an important emotion or new state: friendship, love or sorrow, or the promise of a marriage or a firm union. There are as many styles of rings as there are of wedding: simple bands or exotic rings encrusted with precious gems, plain or decorated with clasped hands, hearts or initials, or engraved with words of love or a motto.

An engagement ring containing your birthstone is said to bring you luck:

January: garnet—constancy, truth
February: amethyst—sincerity
March: aquamarine—courage
April: diamond—innocence and light
May: emerald—happiness, success in love
June: pearl—beauty
July: ruby—love, chastity
August: peridot—joy
September: sapphire—wisdom
October: opal—hope

The Important Day

November: topaz—fidelity
December: turquoise—success

Some may be superstitious about emeralds (bad luck), rubies (blood), and pearls (tears), and others may want to avoid the cliché of diamonds, as seventy-five percent of all women go for an all-diamond engagement ring. There is no denying that diamonds are classic, beautiful, and hard-wearing, and they do have a wider significance. They were once believed to have protective properties: the light reflected from the bright stones was thought to ward off evil spirits jealous of the couple's happiness. Their brightness is a symbol of purity, sincerity, and fidelity, and as one of the hardest substances in the world, diamonds also signify the durability of the marriage bond. They were even believed at one time to have a positive effect on fertility (especially if the stone actually touched the skin), and the Italians used to call the diamond the "stone of reconciliation," convinced that it would miraculously smooth marital arguments.

To give and accept an engagement ring in Roman times (where the custom developed) was a legally binding transaction, signifying that a girl had been pledged to a man and was no longer available. You may believe that the mere act of wearing a wedding ring is not out of step with modern thought. Think again! Wedding rings have a rather primitive origin. Early man would capture a woman and encircle her wrists and ankles with chains to prevent her from escaping! Another ancient practice involved circling her body with a rope, which would both keep her safe from evil spirits and bind her to him. Even in seventeenth-century B.C. Egypt rings had a supernatural significance, linked by their never-ending band with eternal love. Ironically, the early Christian Church initially rejected wedding rings as relics of a Pagan time, but gradually adopted the practice.

In the past few years it has become common for both the bride and groom to exchange rings, although twenty percent of men (presumably the more traditional ones) still do not sport wedding rings. In Germany, engagement rings become the wedding rings: they are simply moved from the left hand to the right. Jewish wedding rings originally served as a token of the groom's ability and pledge to look after his wife. They were decorated with a house, synagogue, or temple, and were sometimes so ornate that they were not used as finger rings, but as a ring to hold the bride's bouquet. Nowadays they symbolize the sanctity of the marriage bond and tend to be plain hoops made of gold or other metal, sometimes bearing the inscription *Mazel tov* (good luck).

The significance of wearing the ring on the third finger of the left hand is interesting. One rather quaint theory is the mistaken belief that a vein (the aptly but wrongly named "vena amoris") from that finger leads directly to the heart; another is that the left hand represents submission and the right domination—clear messages there!

There is no reason you need to choose a plain gold band as a wedding ring. You might like to consider the traditional Irish Claddagh ring which is used as a friendship ring, an engagement ring, or a wedding ring. It was created in the sixteenth century by a love-lorn Galway jeweler, bereft of his beloved. The design for the ring came to him in a dream: a heart to symbolize love, surrounded by clasped hands for friendship and a crown to symbolize eternity.

Russian wedding rings are a combination of three linked rings, each of a different color gold. They are seen by some as representing the Holy Trinity; by others as symbolizing the bride, groom, and witness. Elizabethans wore a version of this called the Gimmal Ring. Other antique styles of ring include a French Love Knot, a Plaited Love Knot, a Buckle, or a Clinging Ivy. Celtic Knots, Weaves, or Celtic Scrolls are beautiful and often encrusted with diamonds or emeralds.

Victorian betrothal rings include the Pansy Ring in the shape of the flower (pansy from the French *penser*, to think), or the Forget-Me-Not in turquoise and diamonds. Rather in the same way as Victorians used flowers to send secret messages, they would also combine stones together whose initial letters spelt lovers' messages, such as DEAREST (diamond, emerald, amethyst, ruby, epidote, sapphire, and turquoise). Gypsy-set rings were also popular in this period: wide, tapered wedding bands with stones set into the band. Look out for geometric art deco or art nouveau rings, which are both rare and interesting, or square-shaped wedding rings, which are comfortable. Some jewelers depart from the norm with triangular cut or fan-shaped stones.

There is still a sense of magic and superstition bound up with the wedding ring—a symbol of unity, signifying that wherever you go alone, you'll come back to each other again. But rather than a bald exchange of rings, why not place the rings inside large flower blooms and hand them to each other? Or even, rather than exchanging rings, exchange another significant token. One couple in Alaska, both ardent members of the National Rifle Association, exchanged semiautomatic pistols instead of rings.

Choosing a Ring

Here are some things to bear in mind when choosing your ring:

- Go to a reputable jeweler, and remember that you get what you pay for!
- An antique ring will hold its value, and old stones are often clearer and more subtle in color than new ones. If it is more than one hundred years old, however, it will be delicate and should be worn with care.
- Don't be afraid of auctions: prices of rings usually start at around two hundred dollars (although the top ranges are very high!)
- Consider having one specially made, particularly if you have a friend who designs jewelry.
- Gold is alloyed with other metals to make it harder, and the carat number refers to the amount of pure gold out of twenty-four parts of metal. Twenty-two-carat gold is almost pure and the most expensive, but as a result the softest, wearing down more quickly than the durable eighteen carat. It is best to have an engagement ring made of the same gold as your wedding ring.
- The ring should be a perfect fit. If you can twist it round, it is too big. Clean it by brushing gently with a soft toothbrush in lukewarm water with crystal soda.
- Insure your ring.

A RECEIVING LINE

The prospect of a welcoming committee—composed of bride and groom, parents and grandparents—to greet all the guests one by one can be daunting (both for guests and hosts alike). Indeed, it can take up to two hours for large weddings, especially with a toastmaster calling out names! Don't feel bad about junking this idea completely, but remember that although you may be the hosts, you are not really in a position to introduce the guests to each other. If your parents are hosting the wedding, they may also like an opportunity to meet everyone. Even in traditional weddings there is no set time to have the line: as you come out of the ceremony, as you go into the reception, as you move into the marquee. Do make a conscious effort to get round and speak to people if you don't have a line. You invited them for a reason—to witness your vows and to enjoy your day with you. They will want to say a few words to you.

A POSTWEDDING MEAL

Depending on the time of day, space, and funds available, it is generally regarded as essential to have some kind of party after the ceremony. Here are some ideas to choose from:

- blueberry waffles with cream, fruit and coffee
- canapés
- vegetarian buffet
- kedgeree (an Indian dish) with Bloody Marys
- full sit-down three-course meal
- cake and punch
- fast-food (pizzas, burgers, hotdogs)
- picnic
- barbecue
- oysters, caviar, and champagne
- hot bread and cheese

If your wedding is small, you could ask guests to bring a dish each. If you are having a stand-up buffet, make sure there are a few chairs around for elderly guests or anyone who doesn't want to eat standing up.

For celebratory drinks, if you don't want to go to the expense of champagne, what about:

- hot punch
- an exotic pink cocktail: try mixing vodka, sparkling wine, orange juice, and cranberry juice
- fruit cocktails and plenty of sparkling water

- wine: many liquor stores will let you have cases on a sale or return basis and will lend glasses—allow at least half a bottle per head
- or you could always head to a bar or restaurant

If you are doing the catering yourself, you will probably need to rent or borrow tables and chairs, cooking equipment, crockery, cutlery, and an urn for boiling water. Neighbors may be able to lend freezer space.

Some couples have two receptions: one at the time of the wedding, another some days or weeks later—perhaps because many people or important members of the family could not attend the first. It could be a good opportunity to wear your dress again and eat wedding cake once more—but remember that it is a family celebration, not a re-enactment of the actual wedding.

CAKE

Cakes have made a relatively recent appearance on the wedding scene. Dry biscuits were ritually broken over the bride's head until the early sixteenth century, and as eggs, sugar, spices, and currants became more readily available, the biscuits became small cakes—which were still crumbled over the bride's head in Elizabeth I's time. Inspired by French patisserie, marzipan and icing were later added, and with the seventeenth century came the custom for two cakes: sugary and light for the bride, rich and fruity for the groom. These two elements were eventually combined into the traditional iced fruit cake favored by many traditional brides today.

If you want a cake but feel that a tiered, formal, fruit cake, spiky with royal icing, would be over the top, as an alternative try a simple sponge cake, lemon cake, or a mountain of chocolate mini-rolls. Many countries have special wedding cakes very different from our rich fruit cakes and light, sugary cakes. The Norwegians, for example, cook a ring cake made from ground almonds. In Crete they make an elaborate, glazed, bread cake, adorned with birds and flowers. Bear in mind, though, that if you choose a nonfruit cake, it won't keep fresh for as long.

Feeding each other cake and drinking from the same goblet are old traditions that tend to be passed over these days. They are nice symbols of sharing, though, and you might also like to revive the custom of drinking a sour and sweet liquid (vinegar and orange juice, for example) from the same glasses, to represent constancy through good times and bad.

In Spain, silver charms are baked into the wedding cake. Each symbolizes a certain exciting future event, such as a baby, a new house, a marriage proposal, or a tall dark stranger. The charms are attached to ribbons and all the single girls at the wedding are invited to pull them out before the bride and groom cut the cake.

SPEECHES

We've all been there—the ineffably dull round of tedious men holding forth about the groom's laddish escapades or the bride's exploits as a child. This is definitely a tradition that begs to be changed! You could dispense with speeches altogether, but if you have a long reception after your wedding, you may find it good to have a focal point for the proceedings. It is also a chance for people other than the celebrant and the bride and groom to say something in public about the couple, and many couples like to have something said about them by an older friend or member of the family. It adds a formal "acceptance" of the marriage and puts the couple in the context of their friends, family, and former lives.

It is no longer unusual for the bride to make a speech—in a double act with her new husband—but consider also asking the groom's father, the bride's mother, or a close female friend of the bride to do a "best woman" speech. Another alternative would be to ask your guests to offer reminiscences and stories concerning the two of you, or to ask all present to bring a piece of advice for your future together. This might be a quotation, a poem, or a song. At Christine and Mark's wedding, one guest performed a juggling act, as a metaphor for relationships, and another simply gave them badges with "I am loved" on them.

SINGING AND DANCING

Nearly all cultures use singing and dancing as an expression of community and an integral part of celebrations and rites of passage. Many traditional brides opt for a disco, although this can often exclude the older guests. There is, in fact, a huge variety of music and dancing you can choose from, depending on the funds available. Go for a rollicking barn dance; lead your guests in traditional steps—Jewish, African, Thai, Scottish; or see the dawn in with a steel band. As well as music, why not include other entertainment (especially if you have younger guests), such as a moonwalk or a puppet show?

CONFETTI AND "GOING AWAY"

The practice of throwing rice and confetti originated in ancient Greece, when sweetmeats were scattered over the couple to bestow fertility and prosperity. At Malay weddings today, the couple feed each other throughout the ceremony with uncooked rice, and in Turkey guests pin money to the bride's dress. Paper confetti is difficult to clear up and, if wet, can stain clothes, while rice can feel like hailstones! You could also use birdseed, which is healthier for birds than rice, which can kill them. An attractive alternative is a shower of delicate flower petals, so have a friend pass round handfuls of petals from a wicker basket as you leave. One couple chose indoor bubbles, which their guests blew at them as they left the church. Remember, it can feel important for your guests to "see you off" into your future together, so let them know in advance what time you plan to leave.

For a stylish departure, think about:

- pink Cadillac
- thirties-style Asquith Taxicab
- vintage soft tops
- motorbike
- bicycle made for two
- rickshaw
- hot-air balloon
- boat
- waterskis
- helicopter

A helicopter is good for country weddings (there is unlikely to be enough room for landing in town). Look for local air charter companies in your *Yellow Pages* and consult the back of wedding magazines to find companies offering other means of transport.

Fireworks will end the day with a bang, although you needn't leave them to the end: what about just after the ceremony (remember you will need relative darkness) or after cutting the cake? Normally the fireworks would be aerial, but you can choose a balanced display with some pretty ground effects. It is even possible to have a message lit up in fireworks, such as your initials around a heart shape: a lovely surprise for your new husband or wife, or to your guests as you leave. You will need quite a bit of space, about half the size of a football field, to prevent debris falling on your guests or their cars, who will need to be about seventy-five feet away.

You have various options for organizing such a display:

- Purchase a pack of fireworks and appoint a responsible friend to take charge of safety, site checking, and firing.
- Pay a professional firework company to provide the display from start to finish. This option would include insurance.
- Alternatively, the company could put you in touch with a firer who, for a fee, would set up the display, fire it, and clear up afterwards. You would need to be responsible for insurance, although if the display is held on the grounds of a hotel, they may be covered by public liability insurance.

If you are in a urban area or near an airport, it is advisable to notify the police, fire service, and airport as a courtesy. If the display is near the sea, the coastguard should be informed.

WEDDING GIFTS

One of the most ingrained traditions is that of offering the couple a gift that will mark the occasion and remain with them for their married life. It is said that they also represent the breaking of family ties. Usually these gifts are of the long-lasting, household variety. However, if you are older and have an established home, have lived together for a while or are marrying for a second time, you may want something different. Although it would be churlish to turn down an iron or kettle, think about including with the invitations wording such as: "If you wish to give a gift, the bride and groom would appreciate . . ." What you would appreciate is of course up to you, but here are some ideas for alternative wedding presents:

- donations to a charity or a park/woodland trust
- honeymoon vouchers (where a check could be a meal out or a boat trip—get a friend to organize)
- baby clothes
- gifts for your children
- plants or shrubs for your garden
- contributions to a car
- a honeymoon basket (to include champagne, crystal glasses, chocolate truffles, and mead—the legendary aphrodisiac)
- personalized champagne bottles
- food for the wedding banquet

Many gay couples commented on how helpful and courteous stores were in arranging gift registrations, although they were somewhat apprehensive when approaching them. One wedding specialist, on asking the groom's name, was told that this wedding was a little different: they were lesbians. After pausing for a split second, she said, "Oh, that's okay. We can do that, you just have to understand that we can't change the computer program and one of you will have to be listed in the place for the groom."

SPECIAL TOUCHES

Unusual customs from other countries or religious traditions can be incorporated into any ceremony, whether or not you are marrying someone from another country or culture. With their roots deep in mythology, symbolism, and folklore, the following traditions are archaic but charming and could provide another dimension to your own ceremony, as well as delight your guests. Many couples like to retain links with the past as well as create a modern wedding relevant to their own lives. It is a good idea to make sure you explain what you are doing, perhaps in a note appended to the order of service. This will help avoid confusion, especially if audience participation is required!

"Smudging." This is a Native American ritual that involves burning incense or herbs at the beginning of the ceremony. Ask friends or children to pass a container with smouldering sweet-smelling herbs around the assembled company. This is a symbol of purification and preparation.

Flower Girl. Ask a young girl, three to five years old, to strew petals or potpourri in front of the bride and groom as they leave. Adapt this idea by having her scatter the petals in front of you as you process in.

Wine Ceremony. This can be included in the marriage ceremony—not as a symbol of the blood of Christ, but as a symbol of life and the feminine. Both partners may drink from the cup.

Ring of Stones. Thought to originate with the ancient Druids, this tradition has the couple make their vows inside a heart-shaped ring of stones.

Goblets of Mead. These can be exchanged instead of rings, if you want to keep the ring ceremony for another occasion.

Loving Cup (or chalice). This is handed around for all the guests to drink from as a symbolic gesture of togetherness and hope for the future.

Floral "Pooh Sticks." This Eastern European peasant tradition involves the newly wed couple casting circlets of flowers over a bridge to watch them drift downstream together.

Towncrying. You could follow the Romanian practice in which the groom's friends ride through the village on horseback calling out news of the wedding taking place later that day.

Favors. These—usually gift boxes of sugared almonds, chocolates, or potpourri—are given to every guest or a selected few. An alternative to favors are thank-you scrolls, which can be specially printed, tied with a ribbon, and left on the place setting for each guest. Or why not hand out angel (or affirmation) cards to your guests as they arrive.

Loving Spoon. A Welsh tradition in which the spoon, carved out of wood, is presented to the bride by a young girl in traditional Welsh dress, it symbolizes the ability of the new husband to live by the work of his own hands.

Jumping the Broom. This is an ancient Pagan tradition symbolizing the end of an old life and the beginning of a new. After your vows, simply clasp hands and jump over a broomstick or branch.

Throwing the Bouquet. Don't feel you have to throw your bouquet if you have one—you might want to present it to a friend as a gift or have it specially preserved. In France a bride's bouquet is said to be medicinal: three leaves will cure a fever. If you have a circlet of flowers on your head, you could throw this instead like a Frisbee: whoever manages to keep a section will be guaranteed an early marriage! In Switzerland the wreath is set alight, and the brighter it burns, the more luck it brings. Greek brides sometimes wear evergreen headdresses, symbolizing long-lasting love.

Book of Attendance. A relatively new practice is to provide a book for guests to sign—either with just their names, or with a comment, a piece of advice for married life, a poem, or a quote. If you want something special written by each guest, ask them to come prepared. Alternatively, ask people to sign a copy of your vows, or a large sheet of art paper that you can frame later.

Board of Good Wishes. Keep a pin board by the entrance to your wedding and encourage guests to pin their cards up.

Fertility Symbols. Scatter rosemary along the aisle the night before your wedding, use sheaves of corn intertwined with flowers as a decoration, or get a local chimney sweep to come and kiss the bride.

Handfasting. This is a Pagan custom in which both partners bind their hands together with twine or silk for the duration of the vows.

Proclamation. With this custom, the celebrant asks the entire group of guests, or congregation, to pronounce you husband and wife.

Family Traditions. One couple took their first sips of champagne from an antique silver chalice that had been in the family for generations and was always used at weddings and christenings.

A POSTWEDDING TRIP

The word *honeymoon* originates from the ancient northern European custom of drinking honeyed wine or mead as an aphrodisiac during the first month of marriage. It is still common to take a trip after your wedding, although some couples decide to have one *before* the wedding and others invite hordes of friends along. You can also combine weddings with honeymoons (see chapter seven). Quite apart from anything else, a honeymoon provides a wonderful opportunity to reflect on your wedding and your future lives together.

4

Families and Friends

FAMILIES

Even the trendiest of mothers may harbor secret fantasies of seeing their daughters float romantically through a traditional white wedding. Even the most radical of fathers may want to escort his "little girl" down the aisle. Although most parents these days are so relieved their offspring are actually getting married that they are fairly relaxed about the kind of wedding they have chosen, don't underestimate the reaction you might get when you announce your plans for an alternative wedding.

This is what people said:

> They weren't at all sure about the idea at first, but they have come round to the idea and liked the service we wrote for the celebration. I suspect my dad was upset at first about not giving me away.
>
> *Blessing following a beach wedding*

> Both families were very supportive of the decision we'd taken and all really enjoyed the day. As Christians, I think my parents were pleased that we'd done it our own way, in comparison with people who do get married in a church without having any connection with it. One problem was that my parents saw it as their day as much as mine and wanted to invite a lot of their friends. We felt very strongly that we didn't want a huge event and didn't want it dominated by people Tim and I didn't know.
>
> *Nondenominational blessing*

56

Families and Friends

We both come from Christian backgrounds. Our families knew we weren't rejecting this, just choosing what was right for us. They were delighted on the day and very excited by the project. Steve's mom said it was the best wedding she'd ever been to.

Open-air pacifist ceremony

Both sides were very supportive as neither follow any religion. They felt relaxed about their roles in the service and were glad the bride's father didn't have to "give her away"!

Humanist ceremony

Everyone who could afford to come was delighted to combine the wedding with a vacation in the Seychelles. Unfortunately not all our immediate family or close friends could make it.

Tropical island wedding

My husband's family respected our decision, but apart from my mother and one cousin, my family was strongly opposed. They boycotted the ceremony and kept phoning me to tell me that they thought I was selfish and unreasonable.

Viking ceremony

Our mothers would have liked a church wedding, but they were glad we were at least getting married.

Civil ceremony

It was difficult to gauge their reactions at the time. I think my prospective mother-in-law was relieved when we decided to get married, as we already had a child.

Civil ceremony

We didn't invite many family members, just four or five from each side, a reflection of the fact that our friends are much more our "family" now. My husband's family was very supportive, despite the fact that his mother is a lay preacher. They were a little thrown that it was so alternative, but joined in enthusiastically and said afterwards—as everyone did—that it was a deeply moving experience.

Humanist ceremony

My family felt our wedding in Prague was in keeping with my personality, but they were concerned that it all happened too quickly: we met, fell in love, and decided to marry within a month. Jim's parents had reservations because they are orthodox Catholics and our marriage is not recognized by the Catholic Church. In the end, both families were delighted with the wedding, both location and format.

Civil ceremony in Prague Town Hall

With my family, staunch Catholics, religion reared its ugly head. Of the four invited, only two came. The two who did come had converted to the Baptist faith, and were supportive—but both said they felt we would have a more meaningful marriage if we invited God into it. I heard from one of these people that the rest of my family was concerned that I wasn't "properly" married, and in fact two of my more elderly uncles, both priests, have now broken off contact with me because of the wedding ceremony.

Humanist ceremony

Dave was told by his family, "You can't do anything in a normal way, can you?" My father was concerned that our Mexican wedding might not be legal [it was], while my mother just worried about the whirlwind nature of the romance (we got engaged after only two weeks).

Wedding in a hotel room in Mexico City

Roy's family was impressed that he was getting married at all. Mine was a bit confused at first but then very supportive. Both our families supported us emotionally and got involved financially.

Gay ceremony

I had only come out to my family a week before and felt it wasn't the moment to invite them to the wedding, although I shall invite them to the renewal ceremony one year later. Lee's parents are abroad and do not know she is a lesbian.

Lesbian Pagan ceremony

We came up against one set of angry parents, who could not understand our lesbian relationship. They arrived a little uncertain as to what to expect, but did eventually come with goodwill. Siblings, we found, were much more understanding.

Lesbian commitment ceremony

The love, support, and acceptance was greater than either of us could have imagined. The ceremony has made us even more accepted by family and friends alike as a "genuine" couple who are, and want to be, together. We are not just playing at a "pretend" family.

Humanist gay affirmation ceremony

My family was uneasy at first, but by the time of the ceremony they were quite supportive. Their attitude was that we were family and that was all that mattered. At a rehearsal dinner a healthy serving of spirits helped break down barriers and helped them realize that our lifestyle is not much different from theirs.

Lesbian Christian ceremony

My father backed out of coming to the ceremony with a week's notice. I told him that if he couldn't support our ceremony then not to come. I felt that this event was for us and that I didn't want to have to coddle his feelings all night. If people couldn't handle it they should stay away. My mother was adamantly supportive, as was her husband who came to the ceremony but was bothered by male to male affection and left early. My sister came to show her support but was uncomfortable.

Gay affirmation ceremony

Some of our family members were very supportive. Our fathers were not and were not invited, although, strangely enough, wanted to attend. We took a very firm line and said that we only wanted people to attend for the right reasons, i.e. for celebration, not obligation.

Gay Unitarian ceremony

Dealing with opposition or even well-meant but unwanted advice from your families is not easy. Much depends on the type of people you are. You may regard your wedding as a private matter between the two of you, or alternatively it may be something you want to do within the context of friends, family, and community. This will of course affect the involvement you want and expect from your family. Some of those people I spoke to who had dug their heels in regretted it later; others did not.

Before a major family rift develops, take a deep breath and think about the following:

- Remember that your parents probably have preconceived ideas about how they expect your wedding to be. It doesn't necessarily mean they want to impose it on you—just that they have not yet considered any alternatives. There is a huge industry devoted to making people believe they have to marry in a certain, traditional way, so don't jump to blaming your families for being brainwashed by society's expectations.

- Don't present your plans for your wedding until you have formulated exactly what you want on the day. Not only is it important for you two to feel your wedding is your own, but if you appear not to have made up your minds you will be easy prey for a domineering parent who wants to take over.

- Be prepared to explain gently but firmly why you have chosen your particular style of wedding.

- If you are prepared to compromise on any points, decide which ones before discussing your wedding with your family. It is always helpful in any negotation to be able to concede points unimportant to you but apparently important to the other side! And it is nice to be able to include some of your parents' ideas if you can.

- There may be some irreconcilable differences. Try to distinguish between what really matters and what in a few months or years will seem ridiculously trivial. You may regret it in years to come if you have come to serious blows that result in family members staying away from your wedding.

- They may have strange ways of showing it, but your parents do love you and want the best for you. It may help if you try to see their intrusiveness as an expression of their wish for you to have a wonderful wedding.

- Get both sides of the family together over a few drinks sometime before the wedding. You will find that helps break down barriers and eases negotiations (unless you have too much, that is).

- Don't get into blaming or defensive behavior—it will detract from

the excitement and fun of planning a wedding and will sour the
atmosphere.

- Keep your expectations realistic. The day does not have to be a
virtuoso performance. Yes, it's important, but it is just one day. The
most important thing is that you two are going to be together for the
rest of your lives. If you get tied up in family arguments, your day will
not be as happy as it could be.

FRIENDS

With fewer personal axes to grind, your friends are naturally much happier
to adapt to the wedding you have chosen. If your parents are confused or
being difficult, you will need your friends all the more. You may even
persuade one of them to talk to your parents. Low-budget weddings always
tend to bring out the generosity in people, and unusual weddings generate
excitement and interest. You'll probably find all your friends enter into the
spirit of the occasion.

Here are some quotations from couples I interviewed:

My friends were very supportive. Several people said they wished they had
done the same, or would do so. Some were rather confused by the whole
thing!

Nondenominational blessing

All our friends were involved with the wedding—readings, speeches, ushers,
helping with our outfits. Some were a little apprehensive about whether it
would work, but everyone enjoyed it.

Ceremony of blessing and celebration in a garden

Our friends were very curious at first, very interested, and totally supportive.
Several friends with special talents helped out: one made the dress, another
the rings, others made the food, took the photographs, and lent their car.

Humanist ceremony

My friends were great. They organized costumes and helped with the
catering: a medieval banquet.

Viking ceremony

Alternative Weddings

We were quite prepared to marry alone, but several friends insisted on coming to Las Vegas. Some felt a little upset that they couldn't come. In the end we had an international group of friends at the wedding, comprising Japanese, Americans, Koreans, Italians, and English.

Las Vegas wedding

It was a very warm, emotional, uplifting, and overwhelming occasion for ourselves and all involved. It was a very positive act for gay acceptance, to the degree that several gay friends stated afterward that it had changed their perspective on life.

Humanist gay affirmation ceremony

Before the ceremony our friends praised our congruence in having the wedding we wanted. After the event, they praised our sense of occasion, style, and spirituality. We also arranged the wedding so that everyone had a task (driving the wedding car, reading, holding the bouquet) and there was no one who didn't join in enthusiastically.

Humanist ceremony

We had a team of fourteen friends to help in the preparations and the ceremony itself. We invited all the guests to say something at the wedding, which felt very moving and special. Many people commented afterwards that they felt "cocooned in love and happiness."

Lesbian commitment ceremony

For us, the main problem was explaining the ritual significance of a Pagan ceremony as well as the parts they would all play in it. However, we found that, unlike our families, our close friends—both straight and gay—were very supportive.

Lesbian Pagan ceremony

Todd and Michael commented that "as usual in the gay community, friends were the most supportive. Without them we wouldn't have been able to pull the whole thing off." Conversely, Karen and Jean did not find that their friends were universally supportive. "One older homophobic lesbian couple did not acknowledge the invitation and refused to come. A close friend, who we asked to sing, declined. She struggled with whether or not she should and decided not to. She is a conservative Christian and part of her struggles centered around the rigid philosophy of her church." Similarly, Michael notes that his straight friends tended to be more supportive than his gay friends, perhaps because his gay friends, accustomed to keeping the details of intimate relationships more private, still felt uncomfortable about such a public commitment.

The conclusion all these couples came to was: take the time to explain to your friends why you are having an alternative wedding and what it will involve. If you can, let them help with the preparations.

PART TWO

5

The Ceremony

A MARRIAGE represents an ending (of an old life), a coming together (of the couple), and a beginning (of the new life). The ceremony in itself contains elements of all these. It is at once ritualistic and unique, solemn and joyful.

The following pages present a variety of ceremonies from different traditions. The only binding elements of the ceremony are the promises you make to each other and the pronouncement that you are married. You can pick and choose other elements from the different traditions, but here is the most common basic format:

Introduction (Convocation or Charge to the Convocation). The celebrant welcomes the guests and asks them to remember the significance of marriage and to honor the vows the couple is making. Literally, he "calls upon" those present to bear witness.

Opening Prayers (Invocation). If you are having a religious wedding, this is where the Higher Power (God, your own Higher Selves, Mother Earth, or whatever has meaning for you) is invoked to be present at the ceremony. It highlights the gravity of the ceremony and opens it up to wider meanings.

Address. Akin to a homily or a sermon, this is a message from the celebrant both to you as a couple and to your guests—usually concerning the commitment you are making through marriage. You can either let the celebrant write it himself or design it together and include some personal notes. For a gay wedding, this is where you could introduce a political note.

Consecration. A spiritual moment in the ceremony, this is a time for prayers that will underline the sacredness of the promises you are about to make.

Declaration of Consent. The bride and groom speak out loud their intention to marry freely, willingly, and without coercion.

Vows. The key moment of any wedding, vows focus attention on the couple binding themselves emotionally and legally to each other.

Blessing and Exchanging of Rings. A symbolic and spiritual act.

Pronouncement of Marriage. The climactic moment that marks the exact moment of marriage.

Final Benediction. A joyous end to the ceremony as the now married couple is sent out into the world.

The above format omits the traditional presentation of the bride ("Who giveth this woman to be married? . . ."), which, if you decide to include it, comes after the declaration of consent and before the vows. Readings usually come before the address, but you could include readings and music throughout the ceremony if you and the celebrant feel it is appropriate.

We will now look at a selection of various marriage ceremonies from different traditions: some ancient, others modern, some established, others tailor-made for a particular couple. They are printed in their entirety (without music and readings). You will be able to see how they fit, broadly speaking, into the above structure, although some do depart quite radically from it. I hope they will provide inspiration and direction for your own ceremony and enable you to choose a wedding to suit *you.*

THE TRADITIONAL PROTESTANT SERVICE

I have started with this to show why it is not difficult to understand why so many nonbelieving couples marry in a church. Beautiful surroundings, ritual, tradition, solemnity, and a service that embodies ideals and aims that are timeless and relevant: faithfulness, domestic harmony, a mutual love and service, a stable environment for bringing up children, and a sense of the couple's place in the wider community. A few ministers will refuse non-Christian couples; some will expect to talk to you about the meaning of a Christian marriage; but most get on with their duties as master of ceremonies without making too much of a fuss.

Most traditional services date from the mid-seventeenth century Anglican church in Britain. These services include some wonderful, ancient, ritualistic words. However, if you have no sense of religion or do not believe in God, they may feel meaningless, despite their poetry and beauty. In 1928 Church of England authorities made a concession to equality by offering the option to delete the word *obey*. Most denominations in the United States are similarly flexible. However, some people feel that couples who use the slightly more modern wording are still accepting a patriarchal ceremony in which a modestly veiled woman, dressed in virginal white, is handed over by her father to her husband.

It may seem strange to quote this service in a book on "alternative" weddings, but many couples rush headlong into a traditional wedding without fully realizing the import of the ceremony. To help you decide whether or not the traditional church wedding is for you, I quote below the 1980 version of the traditional Anglican Christian marriage service.

MINISTER: We have come together in the presence of God to witness the marriage of (name) and (name), to ask his blessing on them, and to share in their joy. Our Lord Jesus Christ was himself a guest at a wedding in Cana of Galilee, and through his Spirit he is with us now.

The Scriptures teach us that marriage is a gift of God in creation and a means to his grace, a holy mystery in which man and woman become one flesh. It is God's purpose that, as husband and wife give themselves to each other in love throughout their lives, they shall be united in that love as Christ is united with his Church.

Marriage is given that husband and wife may comfort and help each other, living faithfully together in need and in plenty, in sorrow and in joy. It is given that with delight and tenderness they may know each other in love, and through the joy of their bodily union, may strengthen the union of their hearts and lives. It is given that they may have children and be blessed in caring for them and bringing them up in accordance with God's will, to his praise and glory.

In marriage, husband and wife belong to one another, and they begin a new life together in the community. It is a way of life that all should honor; and it must not be undertaken carelessly, lightly, or selfishly, but reverently, responsibly, and after serious thought.

This is the way of life, created and hallowed by God, that (name) and (name) are now to begin. They will each give their consent to the other; they will join hands and exchange solemn vows, and in token of this they will give and receive a ring.

Therefore, on this their wedding day we pray with them that, strengthened and guided by God, they may fulfil his purpose for the whole of their earthly life together.

[To the congregation] But first I am required to ask anyone present who knows a reason why these persons may not lawfully marry, to declare it now.

[To the couple] The vows you are about to take are to be made in the name of God, who is judge of all and who knows all the secrets of our hearts: therefore if either of you knows a reason why you may not lawfully marry, you must declare it now.

[To the groom] (name), will you take (name) to be your wife? Will you love her, comfort her, honor and protect her, and, forsaking all others, be faithful to her as long as you both shall live?

GROOM: I will.

MINISTER: [To the bride] (name), will you take (name) to be your husband? Will you love him, comfort him, honor and protect him, and forsaking all others, be faithful to him as long as you both shall live?

BRIDE: I will.

[The priest may receive the bride from the hands of her

father (though it is not necessary). The bride and bridegroom face each other, the groom taking her right hand in his.]

GROOM: I, (name), take you, (name)
to be my wife,
to have and to hold
from this day forward
for better, for worse
for richer, for poorer
in sickness and in health,
to love and to cherish, (or, to love, cherish, and worship)
till death us do part,
according to God's holy law;
and this is my solemn vow.

[The bride takes the groom's right hand in hers.]

BRIDE: I, (name), take you, (name)
to be my husband,
to have and to hold
from this day forward
for better, for worse
for richer, for poorer
in sickness and in health,
to love and to cherish, (or, to love, cherish, and obey)
till death us do part,
according to God's holy law;
and this is my solemn vow.

MINISTER: [Receiving the rings] Heavenly Father, by your blessing, let this ring be to (name) and (name) a symbol of unending love and faithfulness, to remind them of the vow and covenant which they have made this day; through Jesus Christ our Lord, Amen.

GROOM: [Placing the ring on the third finger of the bride's left hand]

I give you this ring
as a sign of our marriage.
With my body I honor you,
all that I am I give to you,
and all that I have I share with you,
within the love of God,
Father, Son, and Holy Spirit.

BRIDE: [If only one ring is used]
I receive this ring
as a sign of our marriage.
With my body I honor you,
all that I am I give to you,
and all that I have I share with you,
within the love of God,
Father, Son, and Holy Spirit.

[Or, the bride places a ring on the third finger of the groom's left hand.]

I give you this ring
as a sign of our marriage.
With my body I honor you,
all that I am I give to you,
and all that I have I share with you,
within the love of God,
Father, Son, and Holy Spirit.

MINISTER: In the presence of God, and before this congregation, (name) and (name) have given their consent and made their marriage vows to each other. They have declared their marriage by the joining of hands and by the giving and receiving of a ring. I therefore proclaim that they are husband and wife. [Joining their right hands together] That which God has joined together, let not man divide.

[prayers]

QUAKER WEDDINGS

If you are religious but object to formal religious dogma and tradition, you might be interested in the Quakers, with their pacifist, radical, and liberal roots.

Although they are part of the Christian tradition, Quakers use a variety of writings for their inspiration. Also known as the Religious Society of Friends, Quakers attend meetings that are quiet and simple—the only words uttered are by those who feel moved to do so. A Quaker meeting is based on silence, but it is a silence of waiting in expectancy. Through the silence the Friends aim to come nearer to each other and to God. There are no creeds, no prayers, no hymns, no priest, and no prearranged service. The silence may be broken if someone present feels called to say something that will deepen and enrich the worship. In the quietness of a Quaker meeting those present can become aware of a deep and powerful spirit of love and truth that transcends their ordinary experience.

The Quakers believe that the ceremony of marriage should take the same simple, quiet form as the regular Quaker meetings. The bride and bridegroom, in the presence both of local Friends and those specially invited to the wedding, take one another as partners in a lifelong commitment of faithfulness and love. Both husband and wife make the same promise, seeking God's help for its fulfilment. All who are present are asked to help by prayer and support, whether silent or spoken.

You do not have to be a member of the Religious Society of Friends in order to marry in a Quaker meeting, but you may be expected to attend meetings for a few months beforehand and may be required to be registered as "attenders" (this would not necessarily mean you are committing yourself to become members).

Contact the Quaker Information Center (see appendix) for additional information about Quaker tradition and about planning a Quaker wedding ceremony. Because Quaker weddings have no official celebrant, you will also need to check with your county marriage authority to discuss the legal aspects of the ceremony. Some states, such as Pennsylvania, in which Quaker marriages are common, provide two types of marriage licenses: one for weddings conducted by an officiant and one for weddings with no officiant. Other states may have other provisions for such ceremonies.

The marriage takes place during a meeting for worship appointed for the purpose. The couple should go in as soon as they are ready, but it is helpful if the meeting is already settled. At the start of the meeting a Friend will explain briefly the procedure for a Quaker wedding. Early in the course of the meeting the bride and groom stand and, taking each other by the hand, make their solemn declaration of marriage. Importantly, there is no celebrant, with the responsibility placed in the hands of the couple, who marry themselves. Each in turn uses these words, which must be adhered to:

> Friends, I take this my friend (name) to be my husband/wife, through divine assistance (or with God's help), to be unto him/her a loving and faithful husband/wife, so long as we both on Earth shall live.

After this the Quaker marriage certificate is signed by the married couple and two or more witnesses. This certificate is read aloud by the local registering officer of the Society of Friends, either immediately after the declarations have been made or toward the close of the meeting.

Wedding rings play no formal part in Quaker marriages, but many couples like to give each other rings after they have made their declarations.

The meeting then continues as it began with a period of silence, during which anyone present may speak "in ministry." This can be a time when the man and woman concerned gain inspiration and help that continue to be sources of strength to them during their married life. It is also an opportunity for those who attend the meeting to ask God's blessing on the marriage and to commit themselves to supporting the couple in whatever way they can.

The meeting closes after the Elders have shaken hands. Everyone who has attended the marriage is invited to sign the Quaker marriage certificate.

If you are attracted by an exceptionally quiet, plain, but moving ceremony, the Quaker marriage may be ideal for you. There is nothing to stop you from kicking your heels up afterward!

UNITARIAN WEDDINGS

The Unitarian faith is less dogmatic than much of the Christian teachings. It grew up in the Reformation and is a form of Christianity that maintains that God exists in one person only, i.e. the doctrine of the Trinity is denied. Unitarians also reject the concepts of original sin and everlasting punishment.

In a wedding, the focus is primarily on the couple. A Unitarian minister will want to spend a great deal of time with you before the wedding, getting to know you and your partner, your values and beliefs. There is no set wedding "package," although the ceremony does follow the familiar outline. During your discussions with the minister you will be encouraged to talk about why you have decided to marry and what you want the wedding to convey: joy, commitment, love, planning for the future. You will be able to write your own vows, and there is no need to arrive separately or for the bride to be given away by her father.

It is a religious celebration, but some Unitarian ministers are willing to avoid specific mention of God and instead talk about the Spirit of Life. The minister will recommend some readings but may be ready to include your own selections. You will also find that they often take a more relaxed approach to the music you choose than other denominations do.

JEWISH WEDDINGS

The Jewish ceremony includes two elements: the betrothal and the blessing. The groom places a plain ring (traditionally a family heirloom) on the bride's finger, and the bride signals her acceptance of the betrothal. The couple then stands under the canopy (the chuppah) while the Seven Benedictions are recited, which include prayers for the return of the Jewish race to Zion and the rebuilding of Jerusalem. During this they will drink wine from the same cup, after which the glass is crushed underfoot in a symbolic representation of the destruction of Jerusalem and the Jewish hope for its restoration.

CIVIL WEDDINGS

Courthouse weddings have a rather bad image. Municipal and rather dowdy in appearance, they may be efficiently administered, but do appear somewhat soulless. The simplest form of wedding a couple can choose, civil weddings generally follow a standard form of words, although there is no specific format required. Most civil officials allow couples to include their own readings, music, and other elements in the ceremony. As you plan your wedding, discuss your options with the official to determine how amenable he will be to the ceremony you are planning.

A RELIGIOUS BLESSING

If you opt for a civil wedding, want to marry abroad but desire a service when you return, or are marrying into another faith, an additional ceremony of blessing and celebration might be something you would choose. It could take place in a church, a synagogue, a garden, or a hotel, and is essentially a more personal "addition" to an official legal ceremony. The wording of the service would either conform to your religious leanings or could be entirely secular. The following ceremonies were sent to me by the couples I interviewed, were found in books, or are printed with the permission of various organizations. They are intended to be used not necessarily as a formal template for your own wedding, but as inspiration and guidance. Please note that readings and music have been omitted.

&

Katy and Peter (a twenty-eight-year-old clergyman), who got married on a beach while vacationing in Florida, arranged the following service of blessing in their local church for when they returned.

Welcome

CELEBRANT: We have gathered together to celebrate the marriage of Katy and Peter. Marriage is the promise of hope between two people who love each other, who trust that love, who honor one another as individuals in their togetherness, and who wish to share the future together.

It enables two separate people to share their desires, longings, dreams, and memories, their joys and laughter, and to help each other through their uncertainties. It provides the encouragement to risk more and thus to gain more. In marriage, the husband and wife belong together,

76

providing mutual support and a stability in which their children may grow.

We have come together to witness the promises of Peter and Katy in marriage; to share with them in their happiness and their hopes for the future.

Vows

COUPLE: In the presence of God and our family and friends, here I Katy/Peter declare my love for you Peter/Katy, and seek God's blessing on our relationship.

I will continue to love you, care for you, and consider you before my own needs;

I will trust and be honest with you, in good times and in times of difficulty;

I will rejoice when you are happy and grieve when you suffer;

I will share your interests and hope for the future;

I will try to understand you even when I do not agree with you;

I will help you to be your true self and honor you as a dwelling place of God.

In all this I ask for God's help, now and in the days to come.

Exchange of Rings

COUPLE: This ring is a sign of all that I am and all that I have. Receive and treasure it as a token and pledge of the love that I have for you.

Blessing

ALL: In marriage may you be a source of blessing to each other and to all,
and live together in holy love until your lives' end.
May God bless you and keep you.
May God make his face to shine upon you and be gracious to you.

May God lift up the light of his countenance upon you
and give you peace.

Prayers

CELEBRANT: God the source of love
we pray for Katy and Peter.
Give them strength
to keep the vows they make
to be loyal and faithful to each other
and to support each other
that they may bear each other's burdens
and share each other's joys.
Help them to be honest and patient with each other
and to welcome both friends and strangers into their
home.

ALL: Lord, hear us.

CELEBRANT: God of tenderness and strength
we pray now for all who are committed to each other in
love.
May we be fulfilled through our love for each other.
Through our love may we know your love and so be
renewed for your service in the world.

ALL: Lord, hear us.

CELEBRANT: God of peace
your love is generous
and reaches out to hold us all in your embrace.
Fill our hearts with tenderness
for those to whom we are linked today.
Give us sympathy with each other's trials;
and give us patience with each other's faults
that we may grow in the likeness of Jesus
and become more truly ourselves.

ALL: Lord, hear us.
Amen.

Blessing
CELEBRANT:

> The blessing of God
> The eternal goodwill of God
> The shalom of God
> The wildness and the warmth of God
> The laughter and the foolishness of God
> Be among us and between us
> Now and always.

> Amen.

🌿

Alison and Tim (a twenty-nine-year-old airline marketing manager) also had a ceremony of celebration and blessing following a civil marriage. It was based on traditional lines, with vows, exchange of rings, and homily: "We wanted a feel of being part of an ancient rite of passage," they said. Alison's father, a minister, presided over the ceremony.

Tim and Alison met together outside an open-sided tent on a hilltop overlooking the countryside. They made their entrance together, believing that to arrive separately—having been together for more than seven years and lived together for three—would have been nonsensical. The readings were performed by a friend and Alison's sister, and her mother read the address.

Consecration
MINISTER: Alison and Tim have decided to travel the rest of the way together. We are here to witness them commit themselves to one another and to this common journey.

Expression of Intent
MINISTER: Alison, will you walk the rest of life's road with Tim? Are you willing to share everything, your whole life with him as he is with you? Are you prepared to make a total gift of yourself, body, heart, and spirit, to him, as he is to you?

ALISON: I am willing.

MINISTER: Tim, will you walk the rest of life's road with Alison? Are you willing to share everything, your whole life with her as she is with you? Are you prepared to make a total gift of yourself, body, heart, and spirit, to her, as she is to you?

TIM: I am willing.

Vows

COUPLE: Before these witnesses, this is my solemn promise:
to love you and hold you always as my partner;
to stand beside you in good times and bad because my love is so great and your
presence such a miracle;
to be tender with you and fierce with you;
to nourish you with my gentleness;
to uphold you with my strength;
to go with you through all the changings of age and infirmity;
whatever the sorrows or losses;
until we become true spirits in the end.

Blessing of Rings

MINISTER: Spirit of love and truth, bless these rings and let them be to Alison and Tim symbols of unending love and faithfulness and of the promises they have made to each other.

Exchange of Rings

TIM: I give you this ring as a sign of our marriage.
With my body I honor you,
all that I am I give to you,
and all that I have I share with you.

ALISON: I give you this ring
as a sign of our marriage.
With my body I honor you,
all that I am I give to you,
and all that I have I share with you.

Pronouncement

MINISTER: In the presence of God and before these witnesses, Alison and Tim have given their consent and made their vows of union to each other. They have declared this by the joining of hands and by the giving and receiving of rings. We therefore rejoice in their union. Let us show our joy.

Blessing

MINISTER: We pray that Alison and Tim will be blessed and guided in their journey, a journey that we hope will be a long and happy one. Above all, we pray that they will make the journey from selfishness to true love. Whether together or single, this is a journey we all have to make. In a sense it is the real journey of life.

Miranda and Robert had a marriage blessing in Robert's grandmother's garden. They designed the ceremony themselves, with readings from great religious traditions of the world.

Convocation

CELEBRANT: Welcome!
We are gathered here as one, in the presence of God, our Divine Creator, to join in joyful, spiritual marriage Miranda and Robert, and to bear witness to the ever-evolving, transforming power of love.

To receive and to radiate love unconditionally is our highest purpose and our most natural "state of heart." Love is life's sole reason.

Marriage is an embrace of souls. It is a whole-hearted dedication to surrender to love, to trust in love, and to learn by love.

Miranda and Robert request on this day of celebration—and liberation—that each of us gathered here will, forevermore, give freely of our love, our loyalty, and our support to their union.

Let us pray.

Invocation

CELEBRANT: Oh Divine Creator of all this Wonder, we pray that Your Love, Your Light, and Your Joy may flow through us and around us at this time.

Both Miranda and Robert stand before You with heart and mind open and ready to receive Your Divine Inspiration, Clarity, and Truth. We pray that You touch their hearts with Your presence.

May all of us who gather here as witnesses to the marriage of Miranda and Robert be blessed and uplifted. Please be with us, dear Lord.

As we all say, Amen.

Prayer

CELEBRANT: God is Love, and those who live in Love live in God, and God lives in them.

Almighty God, we pray that you inspire us to become ever clearer emissaries of Thy Love, of Thy Light, and of Thy Truth.

Guide us Lord to fill each and every day of our life with ever greater acts of kindness, acts of joy, acts of love.

May this world and all who dwell upon it be blessed this day and uplifted forevermore.

Consecration

CELEBRANT: Beloved Creator, shine Your mighty Light upon Miranda and Robert so that they may give wholly to one another in total joy.

Nourish their minds with Your Wisdom.

Enrich their hearts with Your Love.

Feed their soul with Your Peace.

Give them the courage and inspiration to honor joyfully the vows of marriage they make here today. And may the cherished promises they make to one another uplift in turn each one of us who is here to celebrate with them.

As we all say, Amen.

Expression of Intent

CELEBRANT: Marriage is a precious gift—a lifelong dedication to love. Marriage is a precious teaching—a daily challenge to love one another more fully and more freely.

With this understanding, do you Robert choose Miranda to be your beloved wife and to love her forevermore?

ROBERT: I do.

CELEBRANT: With this understanding, do you Miranda choose Robert to be your beloved husband and to love him forevermore?

MIRANDA: I do.

Exchange of Vows

ROBERT: Before the presence of God, I, Robert, choose to be your husband, Miranda.

Day by day, I promise
to love you and to honor you,
to treasure you and to respect you,
to walk with you side by side, in
joy and sorrow.
Day by day, I promise
to hold you in my arms,
to grow with you in truth,
to laugh with you, to cry with you,
to be with you,
and to love you with all that I am and all that I
shall become.
This I promise you—from the depth of my heart, my mind,
and my soul—for all our life together,
and if it is God's will
beyond this life and beyond the veils of time.

MIRANDA: Before the presence of God, I, Miranda, choose to be your wife, Robert.

Day by day, I promise,
to love you and to honor you,
to treasure you and to respect you,
to walk with you side by side, in
joy and sorrow.
Day by day, I promise
to hold you in my arms,
to grow with you in truth,
to laugh with you, to cry with you,
to be with you,
and to love you with all that I am and all that I
shall become.
This I promise you—from the depth of my heart, my mind,
and my soul—for all our life together,
and if it is God's will
beyond this life and beyond the veils of time.

Blessing of Rings

CELEBRANT: Beloved God, charge these rings with Your Love, Your
Light, and Your Joy.
These rings, with which you wed, are eternal symbols of
individual and collective Oneness, Wholeness, and
Fullness of Life. Look to them, therefore, each day of your
life together for your inspiration and common purpose.

Exchange of Rings

ROBERT: Beloved Miranda, I give you this ring in celebration of my
love for you and as a pledge to honor you and to grow with
you for the whole of our life together.

MIRANDA: Beloved Robert, I give you this ring in celebration of my
love for you and as a pledge to honor you and to grow with
you for the whole of our life together.

Pronouncement of Marriage

CELEBRANT: As you, Miranda and Robert, have promised before God to
give wholly and freely to one another, and to love each

other according to your sacred vows and the exchanging of these rings, it is with great pleasure that I pronounce you—truly—husband and wife.

Those whom God has joined together may God generously bless forever. You may now kiss one another.

Benediction

INTERFAITH WEDDINGS

This is a difficult issue. Many religions will not accept marriage outside the faith, believing that it totally goes against the meaning of their religion and is therefore invalid. Religious families will often do everything they can to prevent it. As cultures and races intermingle, however, it is likely that more and more people will want to form relationships that cross these religious boundaries.

If you do go ahead with a mixed marriage, you will want to affirm and respect the traditions of each religion. It is a good idea to have two officiants, each representing his own side of the family, and to include readings and traditions from both religions. You will, of course, need to find officiants who can accept an interfaith marriage.

It is quite common these days to hear of Jewish/Christian weddings. Indeed, the foundations of the Christian wedding ceremony are firmly rooted in the far more ancient Jewish ceremony. For this reason, it is appropriate to include readings from the Old Testament, and readings from the New Testament that avoid the mention of Christ. There are some noncontentious hymns, such as "Jerusalem," that are suitable, and a nice touch would be for the Jewish wedding prayer to be read (in Hebrew).

Nicola (a twenty-six-year-old attorney), who is Jewish, and Humphrey (a twenty-six-year-old management consultant), a nonpracticing member of a protestant denomination, managed to make a standard civil ceremony moving and meaningful by inserting readings by Kahlil Gibran, Shakespeare, and an extract from The Song of Solomon. They followed the ceremony with champagne and cake for everyone who attended and then held a traditional Friday night supper for both families. The next morning Nicola took part in the synagogue service and on Saturday night they held a party for more than two hundred people, at which she wore a long white dress with flowers in her hair and he wore black tie. Humphrey crushed a glass underfoot after Nicola's father's speech and the traditional blessing. They finished up, of course, with Jewish dancing.

BUDDHIST WEDDINGS

The Buddhist faith developed in India about 2,500 years ago. The constant search is for Truth, or Ultimate Reality, which is found within ourselves. Various yoga and meditational practices lead Buddhists towards this goal. Rebirth, rather than reincarnation, is central to the Buddhist doctrine, in which karma, or the law of cause and effect, is crucial. The five key precepts are to refrain from certain immoral actions, namely:

- murder (which means that vegetarianism is preferred)
- theft
- irresponsible sexual relations
- dishonesty
- drink and drugs

Buddhism is becoming increasingly popular in the West, where consumerism and the fast pace of life has led to a growing sense of "spiritual undernourishment," to borrow John Snelling's term (*Elements of Buddhism*, Element, 1990). Buddhism helps people find their own spiritual path without having to follow a strict religion or strict techniques.

There are now many Buddhist groups in this country. If you are interested in learning more about their teachings or in finding out how to incorporate elements of Buddhist tradition into your wedding ceremony, contact one of these groups in your area. Buddhists often advise newcomers to make a list of things they want to do in their life, and then to try living life according to Buddhist ideals for one hundred days. At least one of you must be a Buddhist to hold a Buddhist marriage ceremony.

☙

Although Buddhism does not have a wedding ceremony as such, there are ways of incorporating Buddhist teachings and readings into a ceremony, such as the one chosen by John (a thirty-four-year-old production electrician) and Janet (a thirty-four-year-old sound engineer). They held a Buddhist ceremony after a civil wedding, conducted by a Buddhist Master with whom Janet had studied for some time. The format was as follows.

Entrance

The couple enters to the sound of chanting: "Nam Myoho Renge Kyo," meaning "I devote myself to Life."

Ceremonial Gongyo

A shortened version of the ceremony performed every morning and evening by those who practice Nichiren Diashoin's Buddhism. It is essentially a ceremony of gratitude, and consists of the recitation of two chapters of the Lotus Sutra, followed by the chanting of the phrase "Nam Myoho Renge Kyo."

San San Kudo: the Saki Ceremony (or the Ceremony of the Cups)

San San Kudo literally means "three times three equals nine." Saki is offered in a cup to the bride and groom, both of whom take three sips. This is repeated twice more, each time with a larger cup, symbolizing the growing unity of husband and wife.

Vows of Determination and Commitment

This takes place in front of the gohonzon (scroll).

Exchange of Rings

Address

CELEBRANT, A BUDDHIST LEADER:

Marriage is without doubt the most important ceremony of life because, although it may seem paradoxical, upon the success of this partnership depends the ability of both husband and wife to give to this world their full creative value as individual human beings. Through their united resolve to create a wonderfully harmonious, yet essentially progressive, unit of society founded upon the rock of their deep respect for each other's lives, they draw out from each other the Three Poisons of anger, greed, and stupidity, which might otherwise afflict their family life with misery for their lifetime. At the same time, through their victory in this struggle, they are able to send out waves of peace and friendship, not only to the community but to the whole country and the whole world.

In the Gosho "Letter to the Brothers," Nichiren Daishonin wrote:

> Women support others and thereby cause others to support them. When a husband is happy, his wife will be fulfilled. If a husband is a thief, his wife will become one, too. . . . If grass withers, orchids grieve; if pine trees flourish, oaks rejoice.

The relationship between husband and wife is the foundation of society because not only do they have it in their power to bring fresh new lives into this world, but also their home and family should be, in the words of our Buddhist teacher, "an open fortress of faith" that is invincible to attack from the outside, yet is open to all who approach in friendship or with seeking minds; a firm base founded upon trust, from which the family can go forth daily into society, shining with the vital energy, wisdom, and compassion that arises from the universal life-force flowing through their lives. Nichiren Daishonin explained it in the Gosho in this way:

> The hiyoku is a bird with one body and two heads. Both of its mouths nourish the same body. Hiboku are fish with only one eye each, so the male and female remain together for life. A husband and wife should be like them.

I hope you will think of these words of wisdom from time to time, especially when difficulties arise to test your fundamental respect for each other, because ultimately it is this respect, based on the dignity of life, that matters far more than the passion of love. I wish you much happiness and fulfilment throughout your lives together.

BAHA'I WEDDINGS

Baha'i is a religious faith founded in the late nineteenth century by a Persian mystic known as Bahá'u'lláh. His followers believe he was the latest in a series of divine manifestations that includes Buddha, Christ, and Mohammed.

The key precepts of their faith are the unity of mankind and the unity of all recognized world religions. They believe in progressive revelation—that is, that Sikhism, Islam, Christianity, and Judaism were all sent by God to mankind via a great teacher at various stages in our history. According to this belief, different social structures in the eras in which the religions developed led to the differences in the faiths. Baha'is strive for equality of the sexes, universal education for all, and a world parliament.

A Baha'i wedding is very simple, pure, and uplifting. You may hold it anywhere and it can include music, readings, and vows of any kind. The structure is also up to you, although it is common to have readings from the sayings of Bahá'u'lláh, or his son, Abdu'l-Baha.

The most distinctive characteristic of the Baha'i concept of marriage is the fundamental belief that marriage is based upon the submission of both partners to the will of God and that marriage is held to be an expression of divine purpose. Baha'is also believe that the aim of marriage is to procreate and that marriage itself provides a "fortress for well-being."

In the Baha'i community it is common to find marriages between people of different racial, linguistic, national, and cultural heritages. You do not both have to be a Baha'i to have a Baha'i wedding, but you do need to do the following:

- Gain parental consent (unless you are estranged from your parents, in which case the Baha'i Governing Body in Haifa, Israel, would need to give permission).
- Have two witnesses and two representatives of the local Baha'i Assembly present at the wedding.

- Both of you say the following words during the ceremony: "Verily, we all abide by the will of God."

ॐ

Nahid and Peter had a Baha'i wedding. Nahid (a thirty-eight-year-old hematologist) is a Baha'i. Although all Baha'i weddings are different, their ceremony provides a good example.

Opening Prayer

CELEBRANT: He is God! O peerless Lord! In Thine almighty wisdom Thou hast enjoined marriage upon the peoples, that the generations of men may succeed one another in this contingent world, and that ever, so long as the world shall last, they may busy themselves at the Threshold of Thy oneness with servitude and worship, with salutation, adoration, and praise. "I have not created spirits and men, but that they should worship me." Wherefore, wed Thou in the heaven of Thy mercy these two birds of the nest of Thy love, and make them the means of attracting perpetual grace; that from the union of these two seas of love a wave of tenderness may surge and cast the pearls of pure and goodly issue on the shore of life. "He hath let loose the two seas, that they meet each other: between them is a barrier which they overpass not. Which then of the bounties of your Lord will ye deny? From each He bringeth up greater and lesser pearls."

O Thou kind Lord! Make Thou this marriage to bring forth coral and pearls. Thou art verily the All-Powerful, the Most Great, the Ever-Forgiving. [Abdu'l-Baha]

Baha'i Marriage

CELEBRANT: Baha'i marriage is the commitment of the two parties one to another, and their mutual attachment of mind and heart. Each must, however, exercise the utmost care to become thoroughly acquainted with the character of the other, that the binding covenant between them may be a

90

tie that will endure forever. Their purpose must be this: to become loving companions and comrades and at one with each other for time and eternity.

The true marriage of Baha'is is this: that husband and wife should be united both physically and spiritually, that they may ever improve the spiritual life of each other, and that they may enjoy everlasting unity throughout all the worlds of God. This is Baha'i marriage.

Marriage Tablet (read in Persian)

Vows

The bride and groom are invited each, in turn, to say: "We will all, verily, abide by the will of God."

Marriage Tablet

The bond that unites hearts most perfectly is loyalty. True lovers once united must show forth the utmost faithfulness to one another. You must dedicate your knowledge, your talents, your fortunes, your titles, your bodies, and your spirits to God, to Bahá'ulláh and to each other. Let your hearts be spacious, as spacious as the universe of God!

Allow no trace of jealousy to creep between you, for jealousy, like unto poison, vitiates the very essence of love. Let not the ephemeral incidents and accidents of this changeful life cause a rift between you. When differences present themselves, take counsel together in secret, lest others magnify a speck into a mountain. Harbor not in your hearts any grievance, but rather explain its nature to each other with such frankness and understanding that it will disappear, leaving no remembrance. Choose fellowship and amenity and turn away from jealousy and hypocrisy.

Your thoughts must be lofty, your ideals luminous, your minds spiritual, so that your soul may become a dawning-place for the Sun of Reality. Let your hearts be like unto two pure mirrors reflecting the stars of the heaven of love and beauty.

91

Together make mention of noble aspirations and heavenly concepts. Let there be no secrets one from another. Make your home a haven of rest and peace; be hospitable, and let the doors of your house be open to the faces of friends and strangers. Welcome every guest with radiant grace and let each feel that it is his own home.

No mortal can conceive the union and harmony that God has designed for man and wife. Nourish continually the tree of your union with love and affection, so that it will remain ever green and verdant throughout all seasons and bring forth luscious fruits for the healing of nations.

O beloved of God, may your home be a vision of the paradise of Abha, so that whosoever enters there may feel the essence of purity and harmony, and cry out from the heart, "Here is the home of love! Here is the palace of love! Here is the nest of Love! Here is the garden of love!"

Be like two sweet-singing birds perched upon the highest branches of the tree of life, filling the air with songs of love and rapture.

Lay the foundation of your affection in the very center of your spiritual being, at the very heart of your consciousness, and let it not be shaken by adverse winds.

And when God gives you sweet and lovely children, consecrate yourselves to their instruction and guidance, so that they may become imperishable flowers of the divine rose-garden, nightingales of the ideal paradise, servants of the world of humanity, and the fruit of the tree of your life.

Live in such harmony that others may take your lives for an example and may say one to another: "Look how they live like two doves in one nest, in perfect love, affinity, and union. It is as though from all eternity God had kneaded the very essence of their beings for the love of one another."

Attain the ideal love that God has destined for you, so that you may become partakers of eternal life forthwith. Quaff deeply from the fountain of truth, and dwell all the days of life in a paradise of glory, gathering immortal flowers from the garden of divine mysteries.

Be to each other as heavenly lovers and divine beloved ones dwelling in a paradise of love. Build your nest on the leafy branches of the tree of love. Soar into the clear atmosphere of love. Sail upon the shoreless sea of love. Be firm and steadfast in the path of love. Bathe in the shining rays of the sun of love. Be firm and steadfast in the path of love. Perfume your nostrils with the fragrance from the flowers of love. Attune your ears to the soul-entrancing melodies of love. Let your aims be as generous as the banquets of love, and your words as a string of white pearls from the ocean of love. Drink deeply of the elixir of love, so that you may live continually in the reality of Divine Love. [Abdul'l-Baha]

Closing Prayer

CELEBRANT: O My Lord, O My Lord! These two bright orbs are wedded in Thy love, conjoined in servitude to Thy Holy Threshold, united in ministering to Thy Cause. Make Thou this marriage to be as threading lights of Thine abounding grace, O my Lord, the All-Merciful, and luminous rays of Thy bestowals, O Thou the Beneficent, the Ever-Giving, that there may branch out from this great tree boughs that will grow green and flourishing through the gifts that rain down from Thy clouds of grace.

Verily, Thou art the Generous. Verily, Thou art the Almighty. Verily, Thou art the Compassionate, the All-Merciful. [Abdu'l-Baha]

SPIRITUALIST WEDDINGS

Spiritualism is the belief that the dead manifest their presence to the living, usually through a medium or a clairvoyant. Spiritualists are a somewhat anarchic group. The National Spiritualist Association of Churches (see appendix) is the main organization, although there are several other independent groups who may or may not be affiliated with a church. Some refer to God; others to the "Great Spirit."

Alternative Weddings

A Spiritualist wedding would normally take the following form:

Welcome

Performed by the cantor (the secretary of the local association).

Homily

Given on a relevant subject by a medium.

Trance

A medium goes into a trance and may give direct vocalization from the "other side."

Fair Witnessing

Various people are asked to give a speech about the partners and the congregation is asked to witness. A medium witnesses for the dead.

❧

The following is the ancient version of a Spiritualist wedding service. Contact the Spiritualist Association of Churches for information about conducting Spiritualist weddings or incorporating Spiritualist elements into your own ceremony, or to locate Spiritualist churches and organizations in your area.

CELEBRANT, IN PRAYER:

Eternal Spirit of life and love, Father of all mankind, who, through the minds and experience of noble men and women in all ages, hast evolved the sacred bond of marriage to preserve the morality and enhance the nobility of the human race, shower upon us we pray Thee, the mighty power of Thy love, and bless us with the helpful companionship of Thy spirit messengers in this sacred hour.

The Ceremony

May the strength and inspiration of the Spirit World be appreciably manifest in our midst, and the sincerity of the vows here made be recorded in the Higher Life.

THE COUPLE, THEIR FRIENDS, AND WITNESSES:
We are come together in the sight of God and the Spirit World and in the presence of this company to join this man and this woman together in the sacred bond of marriage, to impress upon them the mystic significance of the marriage tie, and to seek the blessing of God and His messengers upon their union.

Marriage is an institution in the laws and necessities of our being, for the happiness and welfare of mankind. It has been made honorable by the faithful keeping of good men and good women in all ages. It involves the most tender and lasting ties that can unite human beings in this life.

As was said of old: "For this cause shall a man leave his father and mother and cleave unto his wife, and they twain shall be one flesh."

To be true, this outward ceremony must be the symbol of an inward and sacred union between two hearts and minds, which the church may bless and the state make legal, but which neither can create nor annul. To be happy there must be a consecration of each to the other, and of both to the noblest ends of life.

CELEBRANT:
If anyone can show just cause or impediment why these two may not be joined together in marriage, let him now declare it or else hereafter for ever hold his peace.

I require and charge you both, as in the sight of God and His messengers and remembering your responsibility to Him, that if either of you know of an impediment why you may not be lawfully joined together in marriage, ye do now confess it.

COUPLE:
I do solemnly declare that I know not of any lawful impediment why I (name) may not be joined in matrimony to (name).

CELEBRANT: Who giveth this woman to be married to this man?
Will you take this woman/man for better, for worse, for richer, for poorer, to have and to hold, from this day forth as your lawful wedded wife/husband? Will you love her/him, honor her/him, and protect her/him, in sickness and in health, in prosperity and adversity, and leaving all others be faithful unto her/him throughout your earthly life?

COUPLE: I will.

CELEBRANT: What pledge do you offer that you will fulfil these vows?

MAN: This ring.

CELEBRANT: From ancient times the symbol of the Golden Circle has been the sacred token of oneness, continuity, and completeness; the outward signification of an eternal reality. Do you accept this ring in token of his troth?

WOMAN: I do.

CELEBRANT: You will place this ring upon the third finger of her left hand, and with your right hands joined, thus declare your marriage each to the other:
I call upon these persons here present, to witness that I (name) do take thee (name) to be my lawful wedded wife/husband.
For as much as this man and this woman have thus engaged and pledged themselves each to the other before God and these witnesses (both seen and unseen) I pronounce them henceforth man and wife. May Almighty God send down his richest blessing upon you both, that you may steadfastly perform and keep the vow and covenant now betwixt you made.
This is followed by an address, hymn, prayers, and final benediction.

The Ceremony

PAGAN WEDDINGS

Paganism is a general term for the nature-related spiritual traditions. Its origins go back many thousands of years, to a time when people worshipped the Earth Mother Goddess as the symbol of birth, death, and regeneration. Pagans also worship the nature spirits: the sun, moon, and stars. There are several different practices within Paganism, including Druidry, Wicca, and Shamanism. Druidry is a highly evolved branch of Paganism, which survives still today. The following sections include examples of simple Pagan ceremonies and the more complex Druid weddings. You will notice that weddings in other sections of this book incorporate some Pagan elements.

In her book, *Rituals for Everyday Living* (Piatkus, 1994), Lorna St. Aubyn offers a variety of Pagan rituals to mark various life stages or emotional events. Her rituals are designed to enable us to get in touch with the life force within ourselves and to sense an interconnectedness with all life.

The marriage ritual in her book is an outward expression of the joining of the bride and bridegroom through their "Higher Selves." Ideally, it should take place outdoors, in order to access the energies of the living earth. If not, bring plants into the room.

Set a large flat stone in the center of your space. Place two vases, each containing a flower, on the stone. These vases represent your two Higher Selves. If you are happy working with crystals, place one next to each flower, to represent the earth energy. Finally, put two candles on the stone, leaving space (to emphasize your individuality) between them and the vases.

Around the stone arrange a circle of candles, making sure there is enough room for you and your two witnesses (if you are having them) inside the circle. Any musicians should remain outside the circle.

When you are ready to begin, both of you should light the candles, starting with one on the central stone, moving on through your half of the circle, and ending with the candle nearest the entrance. You then both enter this Sacred Space, standing one at each end of the stone. Witnesses enter the circle and stand behind and slightly to the side of you.

Make a silent commitment to each other, then each invoke your Higher Self to help manifest the love and joy created by this union. Then speak your vows, affirming that your love will not only be directed inwards towards each other but outwards into the world. Affirm, too, that you are each to remain separate individuals who must be complete in yourself in order to achieve a successful marriage. Lorna St. Aubyn recommends reading Kahlil Gibran's poem, "Love One Another."

The witnesses then leave the circle. You both blow out your own central candle and your own half of the circle. Leave the circle together, and dismantle the ritual site.

🐚

Sharon and James held a Pagan ceremony. Sharon, a Reiki Master, married James on Glastonbury Tor in Great Britain. They chose the site because the Tor is said to be the planet's heart chakra. Their ceremony was inspired by the myths and legends of the place, a sense of the oneness of the universe, and the teachings of Sai Baba, who teaches the religion of love.

The celebrant was a Pagan priest and the ceremony went as follows:

Address

CELEBRANT: Angels, magicians, wizards, and all good beings, join with us on this happy day and let this be a day of gladness, thanksgiving, possibility, and great good fortune for all of us, but especially for Sharon and James who are coming together to demonstrate the wonder of love through the celebration of their marriage.

Sharon and James, you are here because separately and for a long time, you have each chosen the path of self-knowledge. You have paid attention to who you are, what your life means and where you are going. But today, this day of your wedding, is the occasion of the shedding of your solitary journeys in favor of bonding yourself with one another, and your marriage, as well as being the state of joining with another human being, is also the union of two people committed to the process of their own becoming.

The Ceremony

Chalices

CELEBRANT: Sharon and James, I give you this healing water from the Chalice Well, so it may let love and compassion, trust and hope, freedom and joy enter your beings eternally.

Hand Joining

CELEBRANT: I join you in the name of Love.

Invocation

CELEBRANT: Marriage is a very special place, the sheltered environment in which we can endlessly explore ourselves in the presence of another and in which we can offer the possibility of the true reflection of another.

Sharon and James have now found one another, and they know in their souls how perfectly matched they are, and that they are choosing on this day of most special days to become for all time the accurate and beautiful reflection of each other's essence. We ask that the vision they have of one another be always informed by the spellbinding, radiant power that first brought them together, and we pray that as they move into the hallowed ground that is marriage they may always hold one another in the light of all light, the love of all love.

For them, out of the routine of ordinary life the extraordinary has happened. They have experienced the delicious stages of romance, to discover the love of substance and depth they are consecrating with marriage today. Romance is play, but true love is intention, and it is their intending to love for life that we are celebrating today. But today is also a celebration for the rest of us, for it is also a pleasure for us to see love in bloom, to participate in the wedding of two people so delightfully suited to one another.

Therefore, Sharon and James, we thank you. You've brightened our day, and showed us that love can bloom, that marriage is a worthy enterprise and that happy, open-hearted people are overjoyed to undertake it.

Expression of Intent

CELEBRANT: Sharon and James, now that you have heard about the magic and the mysteries of marriage, the way it will continuously surprise you, the strength and wisdom it will everlastingly ask of you, do you choose still and happily and in our midst to make the promises of marriage?

Do you, Sharon, want to marry James, to happily hold him above all and have him as your husband for life?

SHARON: I do.

CELEBRANT: Do you, James, want to marry Sharon, to happily hold her above all and have her as your wife for life?

JAMES: I do.

CELEBRANT: Repeat after me please, Sharon/James.

In the name of God and the universe
I (Sharon) take you (James) to be my beloved husband/wife
to stand with you in the bond of the love that binds us.
To honor you, to change with you,
to open the windows of my heart,
to behold the highest meanings of our being,
to learn compassion with you,
to be with you always.
I promise you this with my soul,
from my heart, till death do us part.

And may all your days together be as the stars in the sky, numerous and bright.

[hands untied]

Exchange of Rings

CELEBRANT: Sharon/James, repeat after me:
I give you this ring as a sign and a measure of my love.
From this day forward your every breath
shall be surrounded by my love, today, tomorrow, and always.

Benediction

CELEBRANT: God bless you, beautiful young ones. May the wings of angels uphold you through all the life of your love, may you live forever in happiness with one another. May your hearts be full, may your lips stay sweet. May your love grow strong, may you live long and happily in one another's arms.

Pronouncement of Marriage

CELEBRANT: Sharon and James, now that you have heard the words about love and marriage, now that you have shown us the example of your love and celebrated your union with great joy and happiness, I ask the whole congregation to pronounce you husband and wife. Please repeat after me, we pronounce you husband and wife. You may now kiss.

DRUID WEDDINGS

Druids were magicians and poets, counsellors and healers, shamans and philosophers. In pre-Celtic times in England, Scotland, and Wales they built stone circles and worshipped Nature. Later the Celts blended the inspiring esoteric, mathematical, and engineering skills of these megalithic peoples with their own flamboyant traditions of artistry and wisdom to create the Druidry described by the Greeks and the Romans. Although partly suppressed with the arrival of Christianity, Druidry continued to survive through the work of the Bardic schools and the folk traditions and customs of Ireland, Scotland, Wales, England, and Brittany. Druid practice was revived in the eighteenth century and spread to the United States, where it still continues today.

Druidry is based on a love for the natural world, and offers a powerful way of working with and understanding the Self and Nature—speaking to that level of our soul that is in tune with the elements and the stars, the sun, and the stones. Druids work to unite their earthly and spiritual selves, with care for the planet being an overriding concern.

☙

The following Druid marriage ceremony held for Michael and Jane is taken from Phillip Carr-Gomm's book, *The Druid Way* (Element, 1993).

[The participants form both a circle and a horseshoe, one inside the other. The Druid and Druidess who will supervise the rite enter. The Circle is cast by the Druid and blessed and consecrated by the Druidess.]

DRUIDS: Welcome.

ALL: Welcome.

[The Gates are then opened by those at the Quarters.]

DRUID: Let the Four Directions be honored that power and radiance might enter our circle for the good of all beings.

NORTH: With the blessing of the great bear of the starry heavens and the deep and fruitful earth, we call upon the powers of the North.

SOUTH: With the blessing of the great stag in the heat of the chase and the inner fire of the sun, we call upon the powers of the South.

WEST: With the blessing of the salmon of wisdom who dwells within the sacred waters of the pool, we call upon the powers of the West.

EAST: With the blessing of the hawk of dawn soaring in the clear pure air, we call upon the powers of the East.

DRUIDESS: May the harmony of the circle be complete.

DRUID: We stand upon this Holy Earth and in the face of Heaven to witness the sacred rite of marriage between Michael and Jane. Just as we come together as family and friends so we ask for the Greater Powers to be present here within our Circle. May this sacred union be filled with their Holy Presence.

[pause]

By the power vested in me I invoke the God of Love whose name is Aengus mac

	Og to be present in this Sacred Place. In his name is Love declared.
DRUIDESS:	By the power vested in me I invoke the Goddess of the Bright Flame whose name is Brigid to be present in this Sacred Place. Her name is Peace declared.
DRUID:	In the name of the Ancestors whose traditions we honor,
DRUIDESS:	In the name of those who gave us life,
DRUID AND DRUIDESS:	May we unite in Love.
DRUIDESS:	The joining together of Man and Woman in the sacred rite of marriage brings together great forces from which may flow the seeds of future generations to be nurtured within the womb of time. Within every masculine nature lies the feminine, within every feminine nature lies the masculine. The interplay of masculine and feminine forces when flowing freely in a union based upon true love finds many expressions. This union is truly holy.
DRUID:	Goddess to God,
FEMALE PARTICIPANT 1:	God to Goddess,
MALE PARTICIPANT 1:	Priestess to Priest,
FEMALE PARTICIPANT 2:	Priest to Priestess,
MALE PARTICIPANT 2:	Woman to Man,
FEMALE PARTICIPANT 3:	Man to Woman,
MALE PARTICIPANT 3:	Mother to Son,
FEMALE PARTICIPANT 4:	Son to Mother,
MALE PARTICIPANT 4:	Daughter to Father,
FEMALE PARTICIPANT 4:	Father to Daughter,
MALE PARTICIPANT 5:	Sister to Brother,
DRUIDESS:	Brother to Sister.
DRUID:	Who walks the Path of the Moon to stand before Heaven and declare her sacred vows? [Jane steps forward]

Do you Jane come to this place of your own free will?

JANE: I do.

DRUIDESS: Who walks the Path of the Sun to stand upon this Holy Earth and declare his sacred vows?

[Michael steps forward]

Do you Michael come to this place of your own free will?

MICHAEL: I do.

[Both walk the paths of the sun and moon (clockwise and counterclockwise) around the circle, returning to the East.]

DRUID: Michael and Jane you have walked the Circles of the Sun and Moon, will you now walk together the Circle of Time, travelling through the Elements and the Seasons?

JANE AND MICHAEL: We will.

[The couple walk hand in hand to South.]

SOUTH: Will your love survive the harsh fires of change?

JANE AND MICHAEL: It will.

SOUTH: Then accept the Blessing of the Element of Fire in this the place of Summer. May your home be filled with warmth.

[The couple walk together to West.]

WEST: Will your love survive the ebb and flow of feeling?

JANE AND MICHAEL: It will.

WEST: Then accept the Blessing of the Element of Water in this place of Autumn. May your life together be filled with love.

[The couple walk together to North.]

NORTH: Will your love survive the times of stillness and restriction?

JANE AND MICHAEL: It will.

NORTH: Then accept the Blessing of the Element of Earth in this the place of Winter. May your union be strong and fruitful.
[The couple walk together to East.]

EAST: Will your love survive the clear light of Day?

JANE AND MICHAEL: It will.

EAST: Then accept the Blessing of the Element of Air in this the place of Spring.
May your marriage be blessed by the light of every new dawn.

DRUIDESS: All things in Nature are circular—night becomes day, day becomes night, and night becomes day again. The moon waxes and wanes and waxes again. There is Spring, Summer, Autumn, Winter and then the Spring returns. These things are part of the Great Mysteries.
Michael and Jane, do you bring your symbols of these Great Mysteries of Life?

JANE AND MICHAEL: We do.

DRUID: Then before all present repeat these words.

JANE: [facing Michael and handing him the ring] Accept in freedom this circle of gold as a token of my vows. With it I pledge my love, my strength, and my friendship. I bring thee joy now and forever. I vow upon this Holy Earth that through you I will honor all men.

MICHAEL: [facing Jane and handing her the ring] Accept in freedom this circle of gold as a token of my vows. With it I pledge my love, my strength, and my friendship. I bring thee joy now and forever. I vow in the face of Heaven that through you I will honor all women.

JANE: In the name of Brigid I bring you the warmth of my heart. [Jane is handed a lighted taper by her mother or female participant.]

MICHAEL: In the name of Aengus mac Og I bring you the light of my love. [Michael is handed a lighted taper by his father or male participant.]
[Both light a single candle together—this candle could be kept and relit at each anniversary.]

ALL: May the warmth and the light of your union be blessed.

DRUID: Do you swear upon the Sword of Justice to keep sacred your vows?

JANE AND MICHAEL: We swear.

DRUIDESS: Then seal your promise with a kiss.

DRUID: Beneficent spirits and souls of our ancestors, accept the union of your children. Help them, guide them, protect and bless their home and the children born of their union. May their life together reflect the harmony of all life in its perfect union. May they work together in times of ease and times of hardship, knowing that they are truly blessed. From this time forth you walk together along life's path; may your way be blessed.
[Jane and Michael walk together sunwise around the circle to be greeted by each of the participants, then stand together west of center.]

DRUID: It is the hour of recall. As the fire dies down let it be relit in your hearts. May your memories hold what the eye and ear have gained.

DRUIDESS: We thank the powers of Love and Peace

for their presence within this Sacred Place. Let us offer the words that unite all Druids:

> Grant, O God/dess, thy Protection
> And in Protection, Strength
> And in Strength, Understanding
> And in Understanding, Knowledge
> And in Knowledge, the Knowledge of Justice
> And in the Knowledge of Justice, the Love of it
> And in the Love of it, The Love of all Existences
> And in the Love of all Existences, the Love of the God/dess and all Goodness.

DRUID: Let the spirits of the Four Directions be thanked for their blessings.

EAST: In the name of the hawk of dawn and of the Element Air, we thank the powers of the East.

WEST: In the name of the salmon of wisdom and the Element of Water we thank the powers of the West.

SOUTH: In the name of the great stag and of the Element of Fire, we thank the powers of the South.

NORTH: In the name of the great bear of the starry heavens and of the Element of Earth, we thank the powers of the North.

DRUID: May the blessing of the Uncreated one, of her Daughter/his Son the Created Word and of the Spirit that is the Inspirer be always with us. May the world be filled with harmony and light.

DRUIDESS: Let us now form the Three Circles of Existence.
[The married couple hold hands, forming the central circle. The participants in the outer circle and the horseshoe hold hands to form two further circles.]

ALL: We swear by peace and love to stand
Heart to heart and hand in hand
Mark O Spirit and hear us now
Confirming this our Sacred Vow.

DRUID: This sacred rite of marriage ends in peace, as in peace it began. Let us withdraw, holding peace and love in our hearts until we meet again.
[The Druid unwinds the circle and exits with the Druidess sunwise. Michael and Jane follow. Then the rest of the inner circle. Then the outer circle walk across the center in pairs and out through the western gate.]

HUMANIST WEDDINGS

If you want a meaningful, nonreligious ceremony, a Humanist wedding is ideal. Humanism is a view of life that has its roots in the teachings of ancient Greek and Chinese philosophy. It is based on the belief that human problems can be solved only by human beings and not by reliance on some supposed supernatural force. Since Humanists are agnostic or atheist, they believe in the scientific explanation for human existence, namely evolution. Their overriding concern is for human dignity and welfare, the ultimate aim being happiness and fulfilment. There is no "book of rules" as such, but in common with many religions they support the golden rule: *Do as you would be done by.* Humanists believe that religions and ideologies are not replacements for the need to take responsibility for our actions as human beings.

Humanists look on marriage as a commitment that involves mutual love and respect. Each party has a responsibility for the welfare of the other, and to the success of the relationship. Where a couple has children, the commitment involves a shared responsibility for their well-being and development. . . . The close and loving relationship of two human beings that is the central feature of marriage lies right at the heart of Humanism.

To Love and to Cherish (Jane Wynne Willson, British Humanist Association, 1988)

Humanist weddings offer advantages to many people:

- They are nonreligious.
- They illuminate important values and beliefs while giving expression to two people's personalities.
- They accord equal status to men and women.
- They have a flexible approach to unconventional situations.
- They allow couples to choose their own words and readings, so that no two ceremonies are the same.
- They suit people who look beyond themselves and their family to express a wider concern for humanity.
- They can take place indoors or outdoors.
- They can include the couple's children.
- They are appropriate for gay couples.
- They provide a popular alternative to the traditional church/civil ceremony.

For these reasons, Humanist wedding ceremonies are becoming increasingly popular. Contact the American Humanist Association (see appendix) for information regarding Humanist wedding ceremonies. The AHA should be able to provide information and additional resources that address the concerns of same-sex couples as well (see chapter 6). As Christine says, "If you aren't totally convinced by a church wedding, go for a Humanist one. It has to be a better deal and one you will ultimately get more out of." Diane (a twenty-five-year-old teacher) and Simon (a twenty-five-year-old journalist) said:

Neither of us is religious and we felt that a civil ceremony was too formal and dull. We wanted to celebrate in a more personal way, and after reading the Humanist documents, we felt that Humanism best expressed our reasons for marrying and our beliefs about society. We wanted a straightforward ceremony without any pomp or religion, so that we could feel relaxed and that the ceremony was relevant to us. We also wanted to marry in the place we met. If we hadn't discovered the Humanist ceremony, we would simply have celebrated by having a party.

Christine added:

When we originally decided to marry, we [almost] settled for a courthouse wedding plus a wild party. Then I heard on the radio that the Humanist Association supported people wanting to hold nonreligious rituals and phoned them. From then on it was easy. They expounded at length on the phone about the joys of alternative ceremonies, got us all fired up about different settings and ceremonies, and told us just how to go about it. Their booklet set out the basics and we took it from there.

Practical Steps

Find a celebrant. The Humanist Association will give you a list of celebrants in your area, or you may have a friend who could perform the role for you. If you want to hold your ceremony in a church or chapel, you will need to find a minister who is prepared to conduct a nonreligious ceremony. Unitarian ministers can often be more flexible (see pages 74–5). Be careful in your choice of celebrant to guide you through the procedure of designing, arranging, and holding your Humanist ceremony. Celebrants come from all walks of life and tend to have a flexible, nonpreachy, and open approach. They often work on a voluntary basis. Christine and Mark adopted a businesslike approach and interviewed three, considering each option and narrowing down their choice. They chose someone of their own age, outlook, and values, who had experience making a ritual work. Others prefer an older celebrant who will appear to be a "wise figure." The fee will vary according to the amount of time the celebrant spends with you.

Compose your vows and choose the music and readings. Because there is no fixed format, you are at liberty to design the entire ceremony yourself. Your celebrant will be able to offer help and suggestions, and it is preferred that you include readings about human love and the family.

Arrange details of time, place, and format. Check that the celebrant can be there, and decide on the format of the party, if you are having one. It is usually a good idea to have a rehearsal the day before, to ensure everything goes smoothly on the day.

If you are concerned, consult your celebrant and your local county authority to determine what you must do to ensure your ceremony will be legal.

The Humanist Ceremony

Humanist ceremonies do have form and structure and convey a sense of occasion. This, in brief, is the basic format:

Introduction

Usually, this involves the celebrant giving some background to the act of Humanist marriage and the couple themselves.

Vows

Called "aspirations" in Humanist terminology, the vows must include the following words to be legal:

"I do solemnly declare that I know not of any lawful impediment why I (name) may not be joined in matrimony to (name); and I call upon these persons here present to witness that I (name) do take thee (name) to be my lawful wedded husband/wife.

Congratulations and Address

The vows can be adapted and readings and poems added.

Christine and Mark held five meetings with their celebrant, Simon, before the wedding, and exchanged faxed versions of the ceremony as they developed it. On the day, he arrived with the final version neatly bound and presented it to them after the ceremony.

Christine and Mark felt that the whole event was a ceremony, with the party afterward an integral part of the ritual. Their ceremony took a circular format, the celebrant at one end flanked by Christine and her supporter, and on his other side Mark and his supporter. The full ceremony, not printed here, included several readings specially chosen to illuminate each vow. The ceremony commenced as follows:

Welcome

CELEBRANT: Good afternoon, my name is Simon Allen and I am here to help Christine and Mark at this pivotal moment in their lives. Although I am a stranger to you all, I hope that you will accept my good intentions toward your friends.

Opening of Ceremony

CELEBRANT: Christine and Mark have already attended a civil wedding for the benefit of the law. Now we are all part of their wedding ceremony for the benefit of them and, indeed, you all.

They wish to declare their commitment to one another in this personal and individual way. For them, marriage is not about how other people have arranged and conducted their marriages and lives. It is about their marriage and how they will conduct their lives.

You might be wondering why you are here and why we are here? If they are married in law, is that not enough? Not really; the law cannot encompass the warmth and affection, the shared experiences that have brought Christine and Mark together, or the dreams and sense of fun that they expect will keep them together. So if they wanted to say something special to each other—why all of this? Well, the answer to that is you.

They could have stood in the kitchen any Thursday night they chose and say most of what they are going to say today—but you would not have been there. So you might have thought that you were here because of them. In truth, they are here because of you. They want and need you to share this with them. You are not here as an audience. Your presence is an intimate part of this ceremony. You are not present to hear recited words. You are to listen to the taking of vows. You are not here to watch a show. You will witness their rite of passage.

The Ceremony

Vows

CELEBRANT: In most wedding ceremonies, the vows form a vital but only small part of the proceedings. Today, the vows—or should I say marriage contract—is the proceedings! There are five vows contained in this contract. Each will be illustrated by a reading from one of us, and then affirmed by Christine and Mark. The function of this contract is that Christine and Mark will take each other as husband and wife, in order to share their joys and sorrows in their day-to-day existence, and in order to pursue spiritual growth through each other's inspiration.

    The first vow is that they will promise to love, honor and cherish each other for the rest of their lives, whatever the circumstances.

[Christine and Mark step forward and make the vow and then return to the circle.]

The second vow is that they will promise to share their work, their home, and their bed.

The third vow is that they will promise to always be willing to negotiate.

The fourth vow is that they will promise to be honest with each other, in thought, word and deed.

The fifth and final vow is that they will promise neither to compromise with each other nor to be timid as they seek a glorious future together.

Confirmation from Witnesses

CELEBRANT: I call upon Melanie and Brian to confirm that they have duly witnessed the taking of these vows.

MELANIE: I do confirm that I have duly witnessed these vows.

BRIAN: I do confirm that I have duly witnessed these vows.
[Melanie and Brian return to the circle.]

The Rings

MARK: By accepting your ring, I affirm my love for you and my lifelong commitment to be your husband.

113

CHRISTINE: By accepting your ring, I affirm my love for you and my lifelong commitment to be your wife.

CELEBRANT: In the presence of this assembly that has witnessed your words, I declare you husband and wife.

Closing Address by Celebrant

VIKING WEDDINGS

The basic format of a Viking wedding is very simple: the groom approaches the woman's father or guardian and makes an offer for her. The groom's family must agree to pay a "bride price" and the bride's family must give a dowry (the more the better, as family honor is at stake). The money is to be invested for use by the couple and is to ensure financial security for her and her children in the case of a divorce (provided her husband is at fault). Terms of the marriage are negotiated and a date is fixed for the wedding.

Guests sit arranged in three groups. At one end of the room are the women from both families. They are flanked on their left by the men from the groom's family, and on their right by the bride's male relatives. The ceremony consists of the handing over of the bride price and dowry in front of three witnesses, and then a banquet is held, with musical entertainment between each course. Because no one with the authority of the state officiates the ceremony, you will need to contact your local county authority to determine what you must do to make the ceremony legal. You may have to conduct a separate civil ceremony later.

Nicola and Alasdair's interest in Viking society grew out of their involvement with archaeology and re-enactment groups, which attempt to recreate the way people lived in the tenth and eleventh centuries. They researched Viking weddings using historical and literary sources, and by consulting a friend who acted as "law speaker" in their group. At their courthouse ceremony the morning before the Viking ceremony, the best man wore full plate armor from the sixteenth century, Nicola a black cloak and veil, and Alasdair a black swede jacket with puff sleeves and red silk lining. Their wedding rings were engraved with Viking runes.

PACIFIST WEDDINGS

Pacifism is a philosophy based on opposition to war and other violence. Although it gained its label in the twentieth century, it is much older than Christianity, and is infused with the teachings of many Eastern religions. Pacifists either work actively toward achieving a society in which war cannot happen or simply lead a life free of aggression in any form.

Maria and Stephen held an open-air pacifist ceremony in a forest. They conducted it themselves, facing their guests. As an introduction, Steve thanked everyone for coming. After the readings they explained their values of pacifism, nonaggression, and vegetarianism. After more readings and songs, they exchanged rings:

MARIA: Stephen, I will feed you. [feeds Stephen a piece of basti, an Indian sweet]
Stephen, I will clothe you. [places ring on his finger]
Stephen, I will comfort you [hugs him]
And I will always love you, Stephen.

STEPHEN: Maria, I will feed you. [feeds Maria a piece of basti]
Maria, I will clothe you. [places ring on her finger]
Maria, I will comfort you [hugs her]
And I will always love you, Maria.

[At this, the couple jumped over a branch, a Wiccan tradition representing the transition from the previous family to a new one.]

6

Gay and Lesbian Ceremonies

DEBATES in the United States over the legality of same-sex marriage have reached a fervent pitch in the last few years, and as discussed in chapter two, remain unresolved. Regardless of the legal issues involved, however, lesbians and gays can still have ceremonies that provide the opportunity to make a public declaration of their love and commitment to each other.

Many organizations, both nonreligious and and religious (including some Christian denominations), foster friendship and support among lesbians and gays and encourage the re-examination of conventional understandings of human sexuality. Whether you want a ceremony that incorporates traditional elements from groups such as the Humanists, Quakers, Buddhists, Spiritualists, or Pagans, or you wish to design a custom ceremony of your own, these organizations can help you take the first step toward planning a ceremony infused with both personal and social significance.

Christian gays and lesbians often have the most difficulty of all in finding ways to incorporate their beliefs into a meaningful commitment ceremony. The Unitarian Church is one denomination that has been both flexible and accommodating with regard to same-sex weddings. Another denomination, the United Fellowship of Metropolitan Community Churches, was formed in the United States more than twenty-five years ago to address the needs of Christian gays and lesbians. Since that time, more than 270 UFMCC churches have been formed across the country, in almost every major city. The churches routinely perform Rite of Holy Union ceremonies for gay and lesbian couples.

🐦

Karen and Jean chose a Rite of Holy Union Christian service of celebration that was conducted at the Cathedral of Hope Metropolitan Community Church of Dallas. Although similar to a traditional Christian wedding ceremony, it omits certain elements that are incompatible with same-sex unions, such as when one person is "given away" as if she were property. It has no legal status, but is not illegal: it simply means that like baptisms, Holy Communion, funerals, and so on, the government has no involvement. Most churches in the United States in which services such as this are performed will usually try to establish that the relationship is long-standing, healthy, and mature. The following is the outline of Karen and Jean's ceremony:

The Charge to the Congregation

CELEBRANT: Dearly beloved, we are gathered here in the sight of God to witness and celebrate the joining of Karen and Jean in Holy Union. This is a special moment in the development of their love. Through their love for one another, their lives have become richer and fuller and they are both made stronger. Having found one another and established their relationship, they have come here to sanctify it and give it special significance by celebrating it here with you in this holy place.

In certain cultures, if you save a person's life, you become responsible for that person. So it is with a Holy Union. As witnesses, we take on certain responsibilities to be encouraging and supportive of Karen and Jean's relationship.

The service is not magic. It will not create a relationship that does not already exist. It is a time for tying the knot in the rope of days and saying, "We will not slip backwards from here, but will go forward together." It is a time for declaring vows and intentions and for facing the uncertainties of the future with the one thing of which they are certain: their love for one another and their desire for that love to last forever.

As Karen and Jean proclaim their love and commitment before us, their family and friends, let us make our commitment to be loving and supportive of them. Let us ask God's blessing on them and offer to them our blessings too.

Statement of Intent

CELEBRANT: The Apostle Paul wrote:
"If I speak with the tongues of humans and angels but have not love, I am but a sounding gong or a tinkering cymbal. Love is patient and kind. It does not envy; it is not proud. Love is not rude, it is not self-seeking, is not easily angered. Love keeps no record of wrongs. It does not rejoice in evil but delights only in the truth. Love always protects, always trusts, always hopes, always perseveres. Love never fails. Now abide faith, hope, and love. But the greatest of these is love."

Karen and Jean, you have heard the Bible's definition of love. It is a high and lofty one, but one worthy of our efforts. I invite you now to state publicly your resolution to live out this kind of love.

Karen, will you endeavor with all that is within you to be faithful to this ideal of love? Will you love and forgive as freely and unconditionally as God loves and forgives you? Will you forsake all others and love faithfully so long as you both shall live?

KAREN: I will.

CELEBRANT: Jean, will you endeavor with all that is within you to be faithful to this ideal of love? Will you love and forgive as freely and unconditionally as God loves and forgives you? Will you forsake all others and love faithfully so long as you both shall live?

JEAN: I will.

Exchange of Vows

CELEBRANT: Since you have both stated your intentions to live together in love, and you have heard the love you profess defined by the scripture, I invite you to turn, and before God and these witnesses, make your vows to one another.

Karen, take Jean's hand and repeat this vow to her after me:

I, Karen Jean Kowalske, take you, Jean Ann Morris, to be my partner in life.

I will cherish our friendship and love today, tomorrow, and forever.

I will trust you and honor you.

I will love you faithfully through the best and the worst, through the difficult and the easy.

Whatever may come, I will always be there.

As I have given you my hand to hold, so I give you my life to keep.

So help me God.

Jean, take Karen's hand and repeat this vow to her after me:

I, Jean Ann Morris, take you, Karen Jean Kowalske, to be my partner in life.

I will cherish our friendship and love today, tomorrow, and forever.

I will trust you and honor you.

I will love you faithfully through the best and the worst, through the difficult and the easy.

Whatever may come, I will always be there.

As I have given you my hand to hold, so I give you my life to keep.

So help me God.

Exchange of Rings

CELEBRANT: Throughout the ages, people have exchanged property as a sign of a covenant between them. In ancient times, a monarch would give his ring to one who represented him, and upon seeing the monarch's ring, all would know that a special relationship existed. In the story Jesus told about the prodigal son, when the prodigal responded to the parent's faithful devotion, a ring was placed upon his finger.

For many years now, rings have served as symbols of a loving relationship. Now Karen and Jean come to exchange rings. As often as you see these rings upon your fingers, may you remember the vows you made today and may you renew your determination to make your love last and your relationship grow.

Let us pray: Bless, O Lord, these rings that as they are given and as they are worn, they may serve to remind us that though we may fail, love never does. As the circle of these rings knows no end, so may the love this day declared never end. Amen.

Ring Vow

COUPLE: With this ring, I encircle you with my love. I present it as a symbol of my constant faith and abiding love. With this ring, I pledge my love to you and give you my heart.

Unity Candle

CELEBRANT: The candle is second only to the cross as a Christian symbol. Early Christians worshiped by candlelight in the catacombs. Almost every house of worship has candles upon its altar representing the presence of God's light.

Jesus said to each of us that we were the light of the world. The miracle of love is that when two lights become one that single light brightens the world more than the two could.

As Karen and Jean come to light this unity candle, we wish them a life together that glows with the eternal light of God.

Liturgy of the Eucharist

Holy Communion

Prayer of Dedication

CELEBRANT: Faithful God, pour down your grace upon Karen and Jean that they may fulfil the vows they have pledged this day. May they reflect your steadfast love in their lifelong faithfulness to each other. From your great store of strength, give them power and patience, affection and understanding, courage and love. We ask, O God, that in every time of difficulty they may find the path to growth and maturity. May all the events of their lives bring them closer to one another and closer to you. May the world be the better for the love of their love.

Hear us now, O God, as we your children pray together the prayer that Jesus taught us, saying "Our God, which art in heaven . . ."

The Pronouncement

CELEBRANT: Listen to the scriptures once more. This is a passage that is often quoted at weddings, but usually they don't note that these words are spoken by two people of the same sex. Listen to the words that Ruth spoke to Naomi. May these words go with you and be yours forever:

And Ruth said to her: "Entreat me not to leave you, or to return from following after you. For whither thou goest I will go, and whither thou lodgest I will lodge; and your people will be my people, and your God, my God. And where you die I will die and there I will be buried. May the Lord do so to me and more also if anything but death parts thee from me" (Ruth 2:16-17).

Finally, listen to these words that are taken from the Apache Ceremony of Love:

Now you will feel no rain,

For each of you will be shelter for the other.

Now you will feel no cold,

For each of you will be warmth to the other.

Now there is no more loneliness,

For each of you will be companion to the other.

Now you are two persons,
But there is one life before you.
Go now to your dwelling
to enter into the days of your life together.
And may your days be good
and long upon the earth.

Inasmuch as Karen and Jean have presented themselves here and publicly exchanged vows and rings as the symbols of their relationship: By the power that is vested in me by this church and by the power of their love, I do proclaim that they are partners for life, in the name of God, the Parent, Son, and Holy Spirit, Amen.

Jesus said, "What God has joined together, let no one put asunder."

You may embrace.

Benediction

CELEBRANT: Bless us now, O God, as we go our separate ways, that the miracle of love that we have celebrated and witnessed shall ever more inspire us to be loving people. Amen.

🌿

Michael and Mark had a Unitarian service that included readings from George Eliot, Corinthians, and the Song of Solomon. These are extracts from the service:

Statement of Intent

CELEBRANT: Michael, do you take Mark
to be your spouse,
to love him and to cherish him,
to help him and to honor him,
and to give him understanding and comfort
in whatever the future may bring?

MICHAEL: I do.

Vows

COUPLE: I, Michael, take you, Mark, to be no other
     than yourself,
Loving what I know of you,
trusting what I do not yet know,
with respect for your integrity
and faith in your abiding love for me,
through all our years
and in all that life may bring us.

Candle Ceremony

[Michael and Mark, using two individual candles, light the Unity Candle together.]

Exchange of Rings

COUPLE: With this ring, and before our loved ones and God,
I promise to stay by your side sharing our
tomorrows and all that they hold, to be with you in
good times and bad, through sickness and health,
and times of happiness and despair. I will always be
faithful to our love and you.

The Humanists have also designed a ceremony specifically with lesbians and gays in mind. The basic tenets of Humanist ideology are set out on page 108–9. Of particular relevance to lesbian and gays, however, is the Humanist belief in the Open Society, in which all are free to live their lives without interference, provided they do no harm to others. As Professor Sir Herman Bondi, President of the British Humanist Association, declared in 1988, "Sexuality is an enormously important characteristic of human beings, which finds many different kinds of expression. To say that we know that only one is 'right' shows a degree of intolerance which I find most objectionable." In 1990, a motion was unanimously carried at the conference of the BHA, to the effect that:

This AGM reaffirms its support for the rights of lesbians and gays. It deplores the hostility directed against them, particularly from religious sources and the tabloid press. It calls upon the Humanist movement and individuals to do everything possible to counter such hostility and to promote lesbian and gay rights as human rights.

The British Gay and Lesbian Humanist Association (GALHA) has been active in promoting equal rights for lesbians and gays in the United Kingdom since 1979. They have devised an "affirmation" ceremony for lesbian and gay couples who wish to make a public statement of their love and commitment to each other. It can take place at the couple's home, a friend's home, or a public place where a room can be hired for the occasion. Although there is not currently a national Humanist organization for lesbians and gays in the United States, the American Humanist Association (see appendix) can help provide information and resources addressing the needs of same-sex couples. They should also be able to put you in touch with a celebrant who will discuss the ceremony with you. Alternatively, you can get a friend to officiate.

This is the basic format of the ceremony recommended by GALHA.

The Entry

In most cases those present as witnesses will be assembled in the room prior to the couple's arrival. The officiant can either stand near the entrance to meet the couple, or stand at a suitable place in the room and allow the couple to approach, accompanied by music.

The Opening

Once the music has stopped, the officiant makes a short opening statement welcoming those present and explaining that they are officiating on behalf of the Gay and Lesbian Humanist Association, which provides this type of ceremony as a service to the lesbian and gay community, and that the couple (giving their names) have invited their friends and/or relatives to witness their commitment to one another.

The Ceremony

CELEBRANT: We have come together to witness the joining together of two lives. In the words of Shakespeare's sonnet:
Let me not to the marriage of true minds

Admit impediment. Love is not love
Which alters when it alteration finds,
Or bends with the remover to remove:
O, No! It is an ever-fixed mark,
That looks on tempests and is never shaken,
It is the star to every wandering bark
Whose worth's unknown, although its height be taken.
Love's not Time's fool, though rosy lips and cheeks
Within his bending sickle's compass come;
Love alters not with the brief hours and weeks,
But bears it out even to the edge of doom.
If this be effort, and upon me proved,
I never writ, nor no man ever loved.
[Replace this with a favorite poem if you prefer.]
(Name) and (name) have come here in affection and
honor to say before us that they will henceforth share their
home and combine in mutual living and responsibility.
Love is the wish of the whole self to unite with another to
the end of personal completeness. Touched by this love,
nature yields tenderness, togetherness, simplicity, honesty,
and delight.

When two people openly and sincerely declare their
affection for each other, they are affirming the precious
truth that love is the foundation of all life—between two
people, between friends, and between all humanity.

I now ask you both [addressing the couple] to speak in
truth to one another and to repeat in the spirit of faithful
engagement these words of solemn declaration that bind
you together. Will you (name) say after me:

I want it to be known to all those present
that I (name)
take (name) to be my lover
and promise to cherish,
love and comfort him (or her)
for all my life.
I offer you this ring

125

as a symbol of our love.
Now together, repeat after me these words:
We have openly declared our love for each other
and do pledge ourselves
to prefer each other's good
from this day forward
and to love and to cherish
in sickness and in health
as long as we may live.
Now we all offer to you (name) and you (name) our sincere good wishes. May you have joy and give joy and make your home a source of strength and happiness to others. I have also been asked to offer you the very best wishes for your future happiness from the Gay and Lesbian Humanist Association. Now, you may kiss each other and sign the Affirmation Certificate.

As the ceremony comes to an end, the celebrant may think it appropriate to lead those assembled in applause, and it is probably best to ensure that whoever is in charge of the music starts it again at this stage.

ॐ

Philip and Steve were keen not to ape heterosexual weddings but used some of their traditional elements to give weight and significance to their ceremony. Both had a best man (who simultaneously handed rings to the officiant); the room was divided into two with an aisle; they read vows, and they cut a cake. Says Philip, "We both took the prerogative to arrive late!" After walking down the aisle together accompanied by music, they stood and faced the congregation.

Introduction

CELEBRANT: Certain people have tried to narrow down the meaning of "family" so as to exclude anyone who is not married and not heterosexual. This attempt is irritating, but in the end, meaningless. We can all create our own family in whatever way we want to. Our partnerships are labeled as "pretend"—we know that there is nothing pretend about the love we can feel for each other, and nobody can take that away from us.

What Steve and Phil cannot do as a gay couple is to have a wedding ceremony that will have any legal meaning. So they have invited you, their family and friends, to witness their commitment to each other, to validate their partnership in the eyes of those who are important to them.

The Affirmation

CELEBRANT: We have come together to witness the joining together of two lives. It is the wishes of Steve and Phil that the words of the next song are listened to, as they have found a "long and lasting love."

Steve and Phil have come here in affection and honor to say before us that they will henceforth continue to share their home and combine in mutual living and responsibility. Love is the wish of the whole self to unite with one another to the end of personal completeness. Touched by this love, nature yields tenderness, togetherness, simplicity, honesty, and delight. When two people honestly and sincerely declare their affection for each other, they are affirming the precious truth that love is the foundation of all life—between two people, between friends, and between all humanity.

Vows

CELEBRANT: Now, [addressing the couple] will you join right hands. Do you aspire to love each other and to live together in a spirit of tolerance, mutual support, and concern for each other's well-being, sharing your responsibilities, your problems, and your joys?

COUPLE: Yes, we do.

CELEBRANT: I now ask you both to speak in truth to each other and to repeat in the spirit of faithful engagement these words of

solemn declaration that voluntarily bind you together.
Will you, Steve, say after me:
I want it to be known
that I Steve
take you Phil
to be my love,
and promising to cherish,
love, and comfort you
for all my life,
I offer you this ring
as a symbol of my love.
Will you, Phil, say after me:
I want it to be known
that I Phil
take you Steve
to be my love,
and promising to cherish,
love, and comfort you
for all my life,
I offer you this ring
as a symbol of my love.

Now the two of you, together, repeat after me these words:
We have openly declared our love for each other
and do pledge ourselves
to prefer each other's good
from this day forward
and to love and to cherish
in sickness and in health
as long as we may live.
And now may we offer to you, Steve and Phil, our sincere good wishes.
May you have joy and give joy and make your home a source of strength
and happiness to yourselves and to others. You may now kiss each other.

Philip says of the ceremony, "Many were moved to tears. Several gay
friends stated afterwards that it had changed their perspective on life."

☙

Of course, you don't have to follow this formula. Martin and Roy held a celebration of partnership after doing some research with the Humanists, Quakers, and Spiritualists. In addition, while vacationing in San Francisco, they went along to the county hall and acquired a Declaration of Domestic Partnership. Their ceremony, held in a forest, was conducted by a straight couple. As Martin said,

> We wanted someone close to us to conduct the ceremony, rather than an unknown person recommended by an official body. We thought of doing it ourselves, but thought it would be a bit like trying to chair a meeting and take minutes at the same time.

After prayers and readings, their vows were as follows:

ROY: Martin, I promise you my love and commitment, an ear for your joys, a shoulder for your tears, and my arms for you always, in all things. I ask you to stand by my side, my partner and lover always. As a token of this bond I give you this ring, for as a ring has no end, so my love for you has no end.

MARTIN: Roy, I promise to love and comfort you, to listen and hear you, and to hold and care for you. I ask you to accept my commitment to you and be with me now, and always. As a token of this bond I give you this ring, for as a ring has no end, so my love for you has no end.

ॐ

Steve (a thirty-three-year-old marketing and public relations consultant) and Mark (a thirty-five-year-old sales manager) chose a Ceremony of Affirmation that reflected their spiritual beliefs, and asked a friend, a nonpracticing Catholic deacon, to help design the ceremony and officiate. It was held at a private home, outside, in the evening.

129

Alternative Weddings

Introduction

CELEBRANT: Good evening. On behalf of Steve and Mark I extend their deepest appreciation and gratitude for your being here this evening to share in their Ceremony of Affirmation, a public affirmation of their lifelong love and commitment to each other.

As a friend, I have had the good pleasure to help them prepare for this ceremony and celebration. And I know that Steve and Mark have put a lot of thought, time, and effort into the planning of this evening. They wanted to ensure that it truly reflects the uniqueness of their relationship and at the same time properly communicates the traditional sense of commitment that is part of any marriage celebration.

You saw this uniqueness tonight when Steve and Mark walked out together, reflecting that they are a couple who is already together, on this their fifth anniversary, as opposed to a couple coming together for the first time in marriage, who start the ceremony apart.

G.K. Chesterton once said that two people truly in love unite themselves in promises. The romantic poet Wordsworth wrote, "Love seeketh not its own self to please, but seeketh out one in which it can be fulfilled." Christ himself, when being asked about the greatest of all Commandments, stated that it was love—love of God and love of one another—and he assured us that the greatest of love is when one person lays down his life for another.

Promises, love, fulfilment, giving your life to and for another. These are not limited to specific nationalities, races, creeds, and gender arrangements. Love is the fundamental essence of building and uniting civilizations, communities, and families. Love is at the core of the human soul that cries out for its fulfilment as a human being. Love of this magnitude is not restricted to love between people of the same color, or people of the same religion, nor is it the restricted and sole property of people of the opposite sex. Love of this nature transcends and soars beyond the boundaries of societal constrictions.

To restrict and limit this love is to suppress the very soul and essence of humankind So what we are celebrating here this evening is unique . . . yet it is not unique at all.

We are witnessing the uniting in promises of two people in love, two people who seek to bind themselves in promises. Two people offering to lay down their lives for the other. Two people who seek to fulfil the other and in turn fulfil themselves.

This ceremony is very traditional, then, because of what it traditionally expresses about love. But it is also unique because it reaches out and proclaims that love between two souls cannot be denied because of the limitations set by a society. This uniting is a magnificent brush stroke on the unfinished canvas of human rights and dignity. This uniting is a movement in the symphonic masterpiece of Living Life. It is that aria from an opera that melodically sounds into eternity. And unless this love is proclaimed and lived, these works of the human soul will never be completed.

Ceremonies and celebrations are vital to the life, growth, and integrity of families and communities. Ceremonies help make the inexplicable explainable. They keep alive the message, the meaning, and the sacredness of human experiences that shape our lives and destinies. Steve and Mark's goals for tonight's ceremony are no less. Your presence as their family and friends gives it even more meaning and sacredness.

The involvement of friends and family within a ceremony is a long held tradition. Steve and Mark's is no different. In place of the traditional bridesmaids and groomsmen, however, they have selected three very important people in their lives: a family member, a friend who knew them before they were a couple, and a friend who has primarily known them only as a couple. We now call upon them to offer witness and reflection on Steve and Mark, as they prepare to affirm their love and commitment to each other.

[Officiant introduces participants, who each say a few words about the couple]

Steve and Mark, you both believe that no priest, rabbi, or public official can marry you. Only you can marry each other. By your mutual commitment to love each other, to work towards creating an atmosphere of care, consideration, and respect, by a willingness to face the challenges that underlie human life, you have made your union come alive.

On this day, you stand somewhat apart from all the other guests. You stand within the charmed circle of your love; and this is how it should be. But love is not meant to be the possession of two people alone. Rather it should serve as a source of common energy, as a form in which you find strength to live your lives with courage. From this day onward you must come closer together than ever before, you must love one another in sickness and health, for better and for worse, but at the same time your love should give you the strength to stand apart, to seek out your unique destinies, to make your special contribution to this world that is always a part of us and more than us.

Today, as you affirm your union, there is a vast and unknown future stretching out before you. The possibilities and potentials of your lives together are great, and now falls upon your shoulders the task of keeping good values and making real the moral and spiritual dreams that mankind has sought. In this way, you will create the meaning of your lives together. If your love is vital, it will make the choosing and acting easier for you both.

In traditional religions it is customary to call down a blessing upon the couple. But I know that you both share with me the conviction that how two people love and treat one another and contribute to the community is more important than any formal doctrine. The two of you, while living out your love, will be a blessing to one another, to those who know you, and to the community as a whole.

132

You stand before us today as two mature and thoughtful people who wish to express their emotions within the framework of a meaningful life together. For your self-reliance, courage, and love, you deserve respect, and it is these attributes that make this a serious—but not solemn—occasion.

I should like at this time to try to speak of some of the things that many of us wish for you. First of all, we wish for you a love that makes both of you better people, a love that continues to give you joy and a zest for living, and a love that provides you with energy to face the responsibilities of life.

We wish for you a home, not a place of wood and bricks, but an island of sanity and serenity in a frenzied world. We hope that this home is not just a place of private joy and retreat, but rather serves as a temple wherein the values of your lives are generated, upheld, and shared. We hope that your home stands as a symbol of humans living together in love and peace, seeking truth, and demanding social justice.

Although we recognize that someday you may or may not have children of your own, we wish for you the joy of the role of parenting. Look upon all your nieces, nephews, children of your friends, and all the children of the world as sons and daughters. Share with them your best traits and values. Your love for each other, against all obstacles, all prejudices, can be a strength for others to learn from. Living in love is the best concept of family that you can share with us all.

Finally, we wish that at the end of your lives together, you will be able to say these three things to each other. Because you have loved me, you have given me faith in myself. Because I have seen the good in you, I have received from you a faith in humanity. Our life together has encouraged me to grow as a person and challenged me to fulfil my purpose in this lifetime.

Steve and Mark have written their own vows and will publicly share them with us all now.

Vows

COUPLE: I promise to love and to honor you
in sickness and in health
all the days of my life.
I will cherish and respect you
and forever be appreciative
of your presence and support in my life
and the strength and guidance you offer
in all my life's endeavors.
I promise to continually offer support and nurturing
to you and your spirit
in your quest for betterment and personal growth.
I vow to always be there to listen and understand
all your concerns, feelings, and beliefs.
I promise to always openly and honestly
share with you and talk with you about
my thoughts, feelings, and emotions
through the good times and the tough times.
Finally, from this day forward
I will be your lover,
your friend, your confidant,
your soulmate . . . and your true companion.

Exchange of Rings

CELEBRANT: Steve and Mark, have you come here freely and without reservation to give of yourselves in a life of partnership to one another?

STEVE
AND MARK: Yes!

CELEBRANT: Will you love each other as true and equal partners for the rest of your lives?

STEVE
AND MARK: Yes!

CELEBRANT: Since it is your intention to affirm your relationship and partnership, pledge your love and fidelity with the exchange of your rings.

STEVE: Mark, with this ring do I pledge my love and fidelity to you for the rest of my life.

MARK: Steve, with this ring do I pledge my love and fidelity to you for the rest of my life.

CELEBRANT: You may now consummate your commitment together with a kiss.

Let us affirm our belief in their love and our gratitude for being part of their lives.

I now present to you, witnessed and affirmed before you tonight, Steve Habgood and Mark Sadlek, true companions.

ॐ

Todd and Michael designed their own ceremony, which reflected to friends, family, and community their commitment to each other, within a nonreligious framework.

The ceremony opened with an introduction given by their best friend, a woman named Alex, who explained the purpose of their coming together publicly. Following this, Todd said his vows, which included a history of their coming together and the life and love they had shared so far. He concluded with his hopes and desires for their future and the depth of his love for his partner. Michael read several poems that expressed his love and feelings for Todd. Alex concluded with a brief closing statement and a benediction based on the universal concepts of love, joy, peace, compassion, and benevolence.

ॐ

Amanda and Avril (a thirty-two-year-old professional organizer and a thirty-seven-year-old psychotherapist) held a commitment ceremony in a garden. They wrote it themselves, using some material from Becky Butler's book, *Ceremonies of the Heart* (Seal Press, 1990). They also incorporated several ancient traditions: Pagan, Goddess, Jewish, and Buddhist.

Avril and Amanda were led into the circle of guests standing under an apple tree. A friend followed, holding two rings on a velvet cushion.

The ceremony started with an invocation to the Four Elements, read by four friends:

East—the Element of Air, linked to the dawn and the masculine qualities of thought and mind.

South—the Element of Fire, linked to the noon and the masculine qualities of spirit, will, sexuality, and home.

West—the Element of Water, linked to the sunset and the feminine qualities of blood, water in the womb, tears, and emotions.

North—the Element of Earth, linked to midnight and the feminine qualities of silence, wisdom, under the mountains.

This was followed by the convocation, in which the priestess called upon the Goddess and the center of the circle.

She then welcomed the gathered assembly and outlined the ceremony. Anointing the brides' foreheads with calming essential oils to purify them from fears and anxiety, she led two minutes "grounding" silence.

The priestess blessed the wine and the bread (two wedding buns) in Hebrew and English. Another friend stepped forward to explain the next (Buddhist-inspired) ritual, the exchange of white silk scarves, a symbol of white light, love, and compassion. Next, poems were read and the rings blessed by a gay friend, who explained the significance of the rings—an outer symbol of inner commitment.

Avril and Amanda then exchanged their vows, each holding the ring cushion:

> I bring myself and my uniqueness to our relationship,
>   and I love you for who you are.
> I promise to follow my heart and be myself—even if it means
>   going into conflict with you.
> I pledge my goodwill to work through conflict or difficulties
>   between us and to get support from others when necessary.
> I promise to be open to my own growth and development and
>   to support you in yours.
> I commit myself to a monogamous sexual relationship with you.
> I promise to make time for myself to nourish my creativity and
>   aliveness and to respect your needs for time alone and
>   with others.

I promise to set aside time to be with you when we can be playful, passionate, sexual, and loving.

I look forward to raising a family with you in our safe and loving home.

The priestess went on to explain the glass breaking ritual (see page 00), and then everyone gathered around the couple for the final blessing, placing their hands on the shoulders of the people in front to form a silent, loving circle.

This was followed by songs, appreciations, and memories from the guests, a toast, and chollah (Jewish milk-based bread), before the circle was finally broken, with thanks to the Four Elements.

Lee and Karen also chose a Pagan blessing. It was held in a friend's back garden in front of a group of six close female friends, a priestess, and several children.

Again, the Four Quarters were important. In the north of the garden they erected an altar, on which they placed three candles, representing themselves and their son, plus a larger candle representing their union, together with their birth stones, water, fire, fruit, flowers, and gifts from friends and family unable to be present.

The priestess, Tarah, began the ceremony by casting a circle in order to consecrate the space. She cleansed the couple with salted water and incense: this helped them move into the circle unburdened by their everyday lives, and to focus wholly on the rite of union which was about to take place.

The friends stood in the circle, four at the points of the compass representing (as in Avril and Amanda's ceremony) Air, Fire, Water, and Earth. Lee was to enter from the East, Karen from the West. To bring them into the circle, two friends each took a candle from the altar and handed them to the couple. Karen and Lee approached the altar and lit the union candle together.

Tarah began the blessing by recalling when and why Lee and Karen had approached her. She spoke of the blessings they had asked her to give and called upon the Goddess of many guises to be there that day to witness and bless this rite of union.

At this, Karen and Lee walked around the circle from the East to the North, receiving gifts and a blessing from each friend chosen as guardians of the Elements. From the East came an image of a bird (Air); from the South some candles (Fire); from the West a water vessel (Water); and from the North stones (Earth). Each spoke this blessing on offering the gift:

> I, the Guardian of Air/Fire/Water/Earth, bestow a blessing upon your union in the name of Air/Fire/Water/Earth and the grace of the Goddess may it be.

This was then followed by readings and blessings read by other friends, and the priestess read a Goddess prayer from *The Spiral Dance* (Starhawk, HarperSanFrancisco, 1974).

Tarah turned to the couple and asked:

> Is it the Goddess you seek to bless your union?
> Is it the Goddess of many names you would like me to call and witness and bless your vows?
> Is this your chosen path?

To each of these Karen and Lee answered "Yes."

Tarah offered a prayer to the Goddess, then Lee and Karen exchanged whispered vows, having decided that they did not wish to share the intensely private and personal nature of their vows.

Their son Jacob presented the two rings for them to exchange and Karen was crowned with a circlet of roses. They offered wine and cake to each other, saying:

> May you never hunger.
> May you never thirst.

The cake and wine were then passed around for the toast:

> To those who were, to those who are, and to those who will be.
> To those who are here and those who wish to be.
> Blessed be.

The couple left through a processional arch made by their friends (who showered them with rice and petals), and then jumped the broomstick.

Karen says, "Traditionally a Pagan wedding lasts for a year and a day, at which point the couple is blessed again. Although your marriage is a commitment that we feel is to last for all time (Goddess willing), we will be blessed each year, and will renew our vows. We both feel that this is a good way to reaffirm our commitment to each other."

ॐ

The stage was set for Tymythy and Norman's trysting ceremony with an altar in the middle of the circle of guests. On it were two taper candles, one pillar candle, and the symbols of the elements: a cup of water, a torch, a cauldron, one goblet holding grape juice, a basket of bread, a bowl of honey, and a cedar broom.

The two high priests wore green robes; Tymythy and Norman wore hooded white robes, and their friends representing the elements wore colors appropriate to each element: purple for air, blue for water, red for fire, brown for earth. Before the ceremony these "element holders" handed a piece of paper to each guest on which they were to inscribe a wish or words of good luck for the couple. The Fire holder lit the fire, and one of the high priests led the couple into the circle from the east towards the altar. Each high priest kissed the couple for luck, handed the elements to the respective element holders, and the ceremony commenced:

EAST: I call the spirits of the East, the gods and goddesses of air. Please join us for this trysting. I hold this sage as the symbol of air. Know and remember that this is the element of life, of intelligence, of purification, of inspiration that moves us onwards. By this sage of air, I bring to your trysting the power of Mind. So mote it be. [Turns back to the circle, walks to the left smudging all that are present. Back at her place, she holds up the sage to the east and makes the sign of the pentagram.]

SOUTH: I call the spirits of the South, the gods and goddesses of fire. Please join us for this trysting. I hold this flame as the symbol of fire. Know and remember that this is the element of light, of energy, of the vigor that runs through our veins. By this flame of fire, I bring to your trysting the power of Will. So mote it be. [Turns back to the circle, walks to the left holding the flame. Back at his place, he holds up the flame to the south and makes the sign of the pentagram.]

WEST: I call the spirits of the West, the gods and goddesses of water. Please join us for this trysting. This cup I hold is the symbol of water. Know and remember that this is the element of love, of growth, of the fruitfulness of the Great Mother. By this cup of water, bring to your trysting the power of Desire. So mote it be. [Turns back to the circle and walks to the left, sprinkling water as she goes. Back in her place, she holds up the cup and makes the sign of the pentagram.]

NORTH: I call the spirits of the North, the gods and goddesses of earth. Please join us for this trysting. This bowl that I hold is the symbol of earth. Know and remember that this is the element of law, of endurance, of the understanding that cannot be shaken. By this bowl of earth I bring to your trysting the power of the Steadfast. So mote it be. [Turns back to the circle and walks to the left, scattering dirt as she goes. Back in her place, she holds up the bowl to the north and makes the sign of the pentagram.]

HIGH PRIESTESS: The spirits are with us, the circle is cast, you are now on sacred ground. So mote it be. [To Norman] Who comes to be joined together in the presence of the God and the Goddess? What is thy name?

NORMAN: My name is Norman.

HIGH PRIEST: [To Tymythy] Who comes to be joined together in the presence of the God and the Goddess? What is thy name?

TYMYTHY: My name is Tymythy.

[High Priests each light a taper candle]

HIGH PRIEST: These two candles represent these two individuals who are here to be trysted. They have chosen to come here today, among all of their friends, to exchange vows and from this day forward be one in union with each other. A trysting is for life. Today, Norman and Tymythy are sharing with all of you their desire to share their lives together as a couple and as friends. May we all listen closely as they exchange their vows.

TYMYTHY: Norman, because I love you . . .

I promise to laugh with you, cry with you,
Talk with you, be silent with you,
Sing with you, dance with you,
Teach you, learn from you,
Travel with you, make a home with you,
Share my life with you, be true to you,
Want you, miss you, need you, love you;
Have you as my friend, my husband, and my lover,
For the rest of my life and all the lives to come.
In front of these witnesses, the gods and goddesses,
So mote it be.

NORMAN: I know you expected me to say "ditto," but I thought I would say this instead . . .

I love you because you know how to bring out the best in me.

I will always love you because when you talk to me, you make me feel special. Your voice is always sincere, always caring.

I love you for the things you say that bring such special meaning to my life. And I love you for the silent times when your eyes and your arms tell me all I want to know.

I will always love you because we share the same interests and values. Though we have our differences, we both have the same expectations of our relationship, both agree on the things in life that matter the most.

On this day I agree to walk side by side together, for this lifetime and all lives to come, in the sun and the rain, in darkness and in light.

I vow to keep you warm and safe.

I give to you my hopes and my dreams to share a lifetime of passion that you may embellish with the love and caring that any good commitment deserves. For I too will be by your side to support and honor your hopes and dreams that

141

you hold close. You are my soulmate. I give you my heart and the love within it. I am forever yours. I love you.

[The High Priests take Norman's right hand and Tymythy's left hand and "tie" them together]

HIGH PRIEST: We tie their hands together with this cord to show that these two have agreed to join their hands and walk together throughout their lives. So mote it be.

HIGH PRIESTESS: Now together, they will light the one candle to show that from this day forward they are two individuals who are united as one. So mote it be.

HIGH PRIEST: As Tymythy and Norman jump over this broom, they leave their individual lives behind and move into the present as a united couple. May only good things follow them over the broomstick and into their future. So mote it be. [North picks up the broom and sweeps away from the couple, around through the circle and out through the east, then returns to the circle.]
The past has been swept away and can no longer affect the future. So mote it be.

HIGH PRIESTESS: [Removing Tymythy and Norman's hoods] From this day forward, Tymythy and Norman are one. So mote it be. Now you may kiss! [Picking up remaining items from the altar] The bread comes from the wheat of the field and represents the abundance of life that Mother has given us. The honey represents the sweetness, joy, and happiness of today and the life to come. As I come around the circle to you, take a piece of bread and dip it in the honey and remember what Mother has given you and how sweet it is to be in this life. So mote it be.

HIGH PRIEST: The grape juice comes from the vine of the field and represents the bitter side of life. Remember that sorrow is a part of life the same as the sweet and that Mother gave us tears to cleanse our souls and fluid to drink to replenish our loss. As I come around the circle to you, take the cup and drink of the bitterness of life. So mote it be.

HIGH
PRIESTESS: Tymythy and Norman would like all of you to take your neighbor's hand and follow them around the circle. When you come to the fire, cast the piece of paper on which you have written your wish for their relationship into the flame. The spirits will see the smoke and know each of your wishes for this couple, and your wishes will come true. So mote it be.

NORTH: Spirits of the North, gods and goddesses of the earth, I thank you for your presence here and for the gift of the Steadfast. I invite you to stay though our circle be opened. So mote it be. [Makes the sign of the pentagram, turns back to the circle, and returns the bowl to the altar.]

WEST: Spirits of the West, gods and goddesses of the water, I thank you for your presence here and for the gift of Desire. I invite you to stay though our circle be opened. So mote it be. [Makes the sign of the pentagram, turns back to the circle, and returns the cup to the altar.]

SOUTH: Spirits of the South, gods and goddesses of the fire, I thank you for your presence here and for the gift of Will. I invite you to stay though our circle be opened. So mote it be. [Makes the sign of the pentagram, turns back to the circle, and returns the flame to the altar.]

EAST: Spirits of the East, gods and goddesses of the air, I thank you for your presence here and for the gift of Mind. I invite you to stay though our circle be opened. So mote it be. [Makes the sign of the pentagram, turns back to the circle, and returns the sage to the altar, placing it upright in the earth receptacle.]

HIGH
PRIESTESS: [Extinguishing the taper candle flames, leaving the pillar candle burning] It is done. Merry meet, merry part, and merry meet again. Blessed be.

[Tymythy and Norman walk around the circle and out through the east followed by the High Priest and the Element Holders.]

143

7

Honeymoon Weddings

ALTHOUGH a wedding at home could cost more than ten thousand dollars, a wedding in Paradise could set you back as little as $2,500.

There are as many possibilities for weddings abroad as there are for dream vacations. Tropical weddings are becoming increasingly popular, with rock stars and actors helping to spread the word. Few people will not have heard about Pamela Anderson in her white bikini marrying Tommy Lee on a beach in Cancun, Mexico; or Michael Praed and Karen Landau's wedding in a hotel in Barbados; Madonna's to Sean Penn on the edge of a cliff; or Christie Brinkley's to Ricky Taubman, in skis, on top of a mountain in Colorado.

A wedding on a ski slope is the whitest of white weddings, and some tour companies are now organizing these. Indeed tour companies in general have been quick to respond to the new market in honeymoon weddings. Many have extensive brochures that cover every conceivable question you might have about vacation wedding packages.

Whether you want to marry on a beach, in a church, or on a boat, there are many destinations to choose from: Caribbean islands, Cancun on the coast of Mexico, Kenya, Hawaii, and the Seychelles and Mauritius in the Indian Ocean are just some examples. White, palm-fringed beaches, stunning sunsets, exotic flowers . . . the appeal is clear. The organization is easy: the tour company or hotel will do it all for you, including the legal formalities, and all you need to do is worry about your dress creasing on the flight over—if you are wearing a dress, that is!

The ceremony itself is very similar to a civil service back home. It is conducted by a local official who will say prayers and words of welcome and who may give a homily on marriage. Some of the words they use can be rather quaint. In Mauritius, for example, the groom might be exhorted to "Love your new bride always and never, ever look upon her as a fleeting pleasure," while the bride might be advised, "And you, sweet lady, must always be very, very kind to your hero." The exact wording varies from country to country, but the vows and declaration of no impediment are essentially the same. You can go as a couple or bring family and friends, but you will need two witnesses.

Nicola and Pascal (a thirty-five-year-old diplomat), who married in the Seychelles, had a civil ceremony in the reception area of a large hotel under a high-vaulted thatched roof. Frangipani and orchids created an aisle, while lush green plants and the Indian Ocean provided the backdrop. Nicola's father escorted her towards Pascal, who then led her up the flower-strewn floor to a small table where they sat and went through the civil ceremony. The ceremony was conducted in French, although the couple made their vows in English. "If the weather is good it is just so romantic," writes Nicola, who now lives in the Seychelles and has seen several couples take their vows on the beaches. "We nearly had our wedding on a small island called L'Islette, which you reach by row boat, but we had too many guests to fit the island!" Catherine (a thirty-eight-year-old attorney) also waxes lyrical over her wedding on a beach in Hawaii: "It was spiritual, exotic, beautiful, remote, intimate, warm, and unusual."

Katy and Peter wanted to separate the legal and religious elements of marriage. They decided to do the legal "bit" on a beach while vacationing in Florida. "The celebration back at home was because we felt other aspects of marriage were important," said Katy. "We wanted to make a public declaration about our relationship and wanted to have a time to celebrate with and include our families and friends."

If you are considering a honeymoon wedding abroad, check the weather for the time of year, if a sunny day is important. In the Seychelles, for example, sun is guaranteed in September and October; December to February, however, your photos may be spoiled by heavy monsoon rains! Bear in mind as well that time differences may cause problems in telephoning people back at home and that laid-back attitudes in other countries may delay responses to letters.

If you decide not to use a tour company, you must find out whether your hotel might be able to help you with arrangements. Determine beforehand exactly what they will be organizing (legal documentation, flowers, food, photography, and so on), and what you need to do yourselves.

You can, of course, go even more alternative than this and hold a ceremony of your own, barefoot and garlanded, in a jungle in Borneo, for example. When you arrive back home, you could simply tie up the legal side at the courthouse. If you want to go even more exotic and marry in a temple in Bali or on Mount Kilimanjaro, I'm afraid that is beyond the scope of this book. Your best bet is to try the relevant embassy or travel agent.

LAS VEGAS WEDDINGS

One popular style of wedding is the Las Vegas "quickie" wedding. Acknowledged by many as the world capital of glitz and tack, Las Vegas boasts a plethora of hotels, casinos, and chapels. Thousands of couples from around the world get married in Vegas each year, seduced by the relaxed marriage laws and ease with which you can get hitched within a few hours of picking up the phone. It's the perfect choice for couples who have been inspired by Nicholas Cage and Sarah Jessica Parker in *Honeymoon in Vegas*, or for those who want to follow in the real-life footsteps of Hollywood stars.

Although you could simply fly there and swiftly arrange the wedding by phone once you have arrived, you may prefer to organize everything beforehand. Marriage licences are issued 365 days a year for a fee of thirty-five dollars, and the courthouse is on the doorstep of several chapels, each with its own particular set-piece charm. If a drive-in doesn't appeal, you can choose from a wide selection that includes a traditional white Victorian-style chapel, an indoor garden chapel, or a quaint country chapel—or even a Graceland wedding chapel with an Elvis lookalike minister . . .

Wedding agencies offer a full "package" including rings, flowers (which you take from a fridge), piped-in music, garter, limousine, photographer, video, champagne, and reception—although you can telephone the chapels and book direct (hotels or *Yellow Pages* will have the numbers). You can choose between a civil and religious service and, if you want to return in ten years to renew your vows, this can also be arranged.

Journalist Jules E. Stevenson was married in the Little Chapel of the Flowers by a "six-foot babe with blonde candyfloss hair and make-up derived from a rainbow summer collection," but does admit that the civil service she chose was surprisingly moving, focusing on friendship and partnership bonding. And let's not forget the economics of a fun Vegas wedding: "Bear in mind that a seventeen-day trip with wedding, flight, and accommodation probably costs less than a third of a traditional wedding on a wet summer day in July."

Sumita agrees: "It was exciting and a chance not to be missed. Another major factor was the unbearable thought of relatives and a boring traditional do!"

ॐ

Sumita and Stewart (a thirty-two-year-old helicopter instructor) married in the Little Church of the West in Las Vegas. They called the Las Vegas tourist board and several wedding services and made their decision based on the packages offered and the price. In the end they plumped for the cheapest at one hundred eighty dollars, which included the service, bouquet, buttonholes, and photos. The chapel was the one where Cindy Crawford and Richard Gere got married. There was no need to book in advance and according to Sumita, "It wasn't too tacky, it had elements of a traditional wedding, and it was over in ten minutes!"

After handing over the marriage license, they were greeted by the minister and presented with a bouquet. The bride and groom marched down the aisle accompanied by an instrumental version of the Righteous Brothers' "Unchained Melody."

"We didn't choose it," insists Sumita. "It made me giggle as it was the music from *Ghost!*"

This is the service they chose:

CELEBRANT: Sumita and Stewart, you have come here today to celebrate the love you have for each other. We share in this with you by giving social recognition of your decision to accept each other as husband and wife. Into this state of marriage you have come to be united.

In man's long history he has never discovered a better way of life than sharing it together in love with another in a lasting and responsible way. This arrangement seems to meet our deepest human needs for love and companionship for someone with whom we can share in an intimate and trusting way all the hopes and joys and dreams of life.

Real love, Sumita and Stewart, is something beyond the warmth and glow, the excitement and romance of being deeply in love. It is caring as much about the welfare and happiness of your marriage partner as about your own. But real love is not total absorption into each other, it is looking outward in the same direction together. Love makes burdens lighter, because you divide them. It makes joys more intense, because you share them. It makes you stronger, so you can reach out and become involved with life in ways you dared not risk alone.

Stewart, will you take Sumita as your wife, will you be faithful to her in tender love and honor, offering her encouragement and companionship, and will you live with her and cherish her as love and respect would lead you, in the bond of marriage?

STEWART: I will.

CELEBRANT: Sumita, will you take Stewart as your husband, will you be faithful to him in tender love and honor, offering him encouragement and companionship, and will you live with him and cherish him as love and respect would lead you, in the bond of marriage?

SUMITA: I will.

CELEBRANT: May I have the rings please? [An attendant hands over the rings.]

Sumita and Stewart, as these circles are designed without an ending, they speak of eternity. May the incorruptible substance of these rings represent a love glowing with increasing luster through the years.

May the Lord God bless these rings, which you give to

148

each other as the sign of your love, trust, and faithfulness.

Stewart, place the ring on her finger and say to her these words:

This ring I give you in token of my devotion and love. And with my heart I pledge to you all that I am. With this ring I marry you, and join my life to yours.

Sumita, place the ring on his finger and say to him these words:

This ring I give you in token of my devotion and love. And with my heart I pledge to you all that I am. With this ring I marry you, and join my life to yours.

And now share with me this brief prayer:

O God, look graciously upon this couple as they share life together, its struggles and problems as well as the joys and blessings, that, in the experiences of life, they will stay close to each other.
Amen.

Sumita and Stewart, you have here promised to share your lives in marriage in the presence of God, friends, and family. Therefore I now acknowledge that you are husband and wife.

WEDDINGS ABROAD

One thing couples who get married abroad often forget is that their wedding will be in a foreign language. If this does not bother you and you're thrilled by the idea of simply saying *si* to an official—go ahead! People I spoke to said it was fantastically spontaneous and great fun.

Not by any stretch of the imagination a quickie wedding, the marriage of Jeanette (twenty-six) and Jim (thirty-one) in Prague Town Hall took six months to arrange. On arrival they were led to a room where an official checked their documents and gave them an eclectic list of music to choose from. Apparently an organist was on hand to play whatever took their fancy, from The Beatles to Verdi. In the end they chose a piece by Smetana for the entrance, "Rhapsody in Blue" by Gershwin for the exchange of rings, and Verdi's "Gloria All'Egitto" for their exit.

They proceeded in pairs, Jim on his mother's arm, Jeanette on her father's, to a large table in the grand, bright town hall. The ceremony was read out first in Czech, then in English. The only participation required of Jim and Jeanette was to state that they had come "voluntarily and of our own free will." After the exchange of rings the translator piped up: "And now the first nuptial kiss, please." The mayoress shook their hands and congratulated them, another official offered them champagne and gave them the cork for luck. The following day the couple returned to pick up their marriage certificate.

This is a translation of Jeanette and Jim's ceremony, handed to them on the day.

> Dear engaged couple, hearty welcome in this lovely, old town hall, where you have come, accompanied by your relatives and friends, to have your decision to live together as husband and wife solemnized.
>
> You are standing here on the loveliest day of your life, which cannot be repeated again, full of love and ideas about your future and faith in the fact that your marriage bond will surpass all troubles and problems.
>
> I wish you from my full heart that this faith and trust may accompany you at all common occasions, even if they are unpleasant, which sometimes may be the case. That is why I also wish you, besides the mutual love, above all mutual understanding, trust and tolerance. You leave your hitherto background and new friendships and relationships will take place.
>
> Now you must build up your new family, sharing common aims. But your ideas and their realization may differ sometimes. At any misunderstanding that may come about, remember this solemn day and all hopes related to it.

Your solemn promise of today not only combines your lives, but is also the origin of the children you will have together. Build up for them something that cannot be bought with any money, the only thing that cannot be replaced by anything other: a harmonious home full of love and understanding. Teach your children to look for pleasure in their lives and to respect higher spiritual values. Give them faith in goodness and hope, in the same way as your parents have handed it over to you today.

This is mainly your day, the day with the capital D, but in spite of this, remember just now your parents. Pay them in your minds words of thanks for their love to you, as well as words of gratitude, because they sacrificed for you all that was theirs. Thank them for trying to teach you the best they could and to hand over a piece of their hearts to you. They know that you will be in need of them even in the future and they are ready to help you.

They know—as you will find out with your own children—that there is nothing more important to a parent, besides God, than the health and happiness of their children, at whose bedside they once sat (and not so long ago), comforting during times of illness and feeling such pleasure when their efforts helped.

Today they have accompanied you here that they may bless your new way of life. And now I may only add a short extract from one of the nicest songs of Jaques Brell:

Come my love, a lucky chance is my shield
and my love will be on guard,
as you are the creature for which I am long sick.
Just now the time is coming for us to love and to live.
Come with me to look for our island —there, far off.
Be happy together and God save you and your
marriage bond!

8

Words of Advice

I ASKED the alternative couples who contributed to this book to offer some advice to other couples contemplating breaking from tradition and "doing it their way." No one I spoke to had any regrets and their words are printed here, as a postscript to the book. May they give you encouragement to follow your own convictions!

It is *your* wedding: do what *you* want.

Be careful how vulnerable you make yourself if lots of people are going to be there.

Say right from the beginning that you are going to do something different and keep saying it.

Follow your heart. Ours was the most beautiful day—many people said it changed their lives. It inspired people to rethink how they would marry.

Consider explaining the background of the wedding to those present. Find some way of making your guests feel just as at ease with the ceremony you offer as they would be with one that they know.

Take advantage of the fact that you have total choice over where, when, and how the ceremony is carried out to create an event that is cohesive, that doesn't break in the middle between ceremony and reception because the church is in one place and the reception in another. That way, the whole gathering—the ceremony and then the celebration—can be one total event and hence more memorable.

Give yourself a long honeymoon; if any kind of wedding is tiring, one where you are so much more in charge of the ceremony and its impact is four times as nerve-wracking and exhausting.

Be sure that it is what you want and the ceremony feels right. Allow others to control the bits they want to.

Make enough time and space to think about the ceremony and vows you really want. Try not to be dominated by your parents.

Expensive or cheap, the most wonderful thing about marriage is the love and commitment to each other you are making.

Do it! Do it your own way, make it your own day that's special to you and your relationship. Don't listen to people who say "it can't be done."

If you have problems with parents, keep calm, try to reason with them, but remember it's your wedding, not theirs.

Make sure that your principles are upheld, but compromise if you have to in order to keep the peace. My parents were pleased we at least had our reception in a church hall.

If you discuss your feelings with your parents tactfully, you will find that they will respect your choice of wedding.

Don't feel pressured by society to have a church wedding. There are so many other more exciting and cheaper ways to do it.

If you're going to have an outdoor ceremony, beware rain and wind carrying your words away.

Don't go for anything too risky or too wacky. The wedding has to be a meaningful ritual for you and for your guests, otherwise you won't feel married. And if you do too much that is risky—helicopter weddings, etc.— then your mind will be on that and not on each other.

If you choose to get married on a Sunday, it will be easier to book musicians, caterers, and the reception venue. But remember that people may have to leave early and not want to sing and dance late into the night.

Don't let family or friends persuade you out of it. You will never forgive yourself if you compromise. Instead, get everyone involved with something to do—they'll forget to fight you over the ceremony and will feel part of it.

Follow your heart and have the wedding you always dreamed of, not what others want or expect or what the law states. You are making the commitment; no one else is.

In a sense it is a portrait of who you are, who you have been, and who you will be in the future. So make sure it is authentically *you*.

Go ahead and do it. Make a stand. It is your life and you should be able to make your feelings and love and commitment known. Above all be positive and believe in what you are doing and why.

Evaluate your relationship beyond attraction and early compatibility. Look at your core values. Are they similar? If not, can you honestly live with and through the differences? This is a commitment, and it should not be taken lightly.

Try to include something that you have always wanted in the service or reception, but if there are things you absolutely abhor that your partner may want to do, please be open and honest about it. Communication is key. If you can make it through planning your ceremony, you can make it through a lot. If you haven't seen the worst in your partner yet, you probably will sometime during the planning of the ceremony and reception.

Remember that even with the best planning, unexpected things probably will happen. If it is something you can change, do so. If not, just go with the flow. It's the unexpected that memories are made of.

Absolutely, unequivocally, *do it*. Having a special day to affirm our love with family and friends was more impactful than we ever dreamed.

Get family and friends together the night before to break the ice and to get to know each other.

Be true to your own sense of what's appropriate for yourselves. Trust your instincts and remember that this is first and foremost for you, not your guests, the "community," or any other authority. The benefit of having a nontraditional relationship is getting to set the rules yourself, and you should have a ritual that reflects your uniqueness. Also, whatever you do, make it sincere. If the words and acts come from your heart, you can't go wrong.

Do it. It was very important for bringing our own relationship into focus. We found we could not really take anything for granted. Our wedding was an extension of our relationship, a concrete symbol. We learned so much about ourselves and our friends and family. We have a stronger relationship now.

Follow your hearts and allow everything to go as it needs to.

I hope this book has helped you to plan a unique wedding day. I have a private theory, completely unsubstantiated by official statistics, that despite the high divorce rates, an alternative wedding—where you are really putting your heart and soul into the words you are saying, the music, and the readings—has a far higher chance of succeeding than a marriage in which the couple values convention and tradition above content and feeling.

I wish you all the happiness in the world and leave you with a poem passed down to one of this book's contributors from his grandmother.

The Art of Marriage

A good marriage must be created.
In marriage, the little things are the big things.
It's never being too old to hold hands.
It is remembering to say "I love you" at least once each day.
It is never going to sleep angry.
It is having a mutual sense of values and common objectives.
It is standing together to face the world.
It is forming a circle of love that gathers in the whole family.
It is a common search for the good and the beautiful.
It is not only marrying the right person . . .
It is being the right partner.

Appendix 1

Planning Checklist

Use this as a working chart to fill in your own details and to check progress.

Time/Date	
Celebrant (minister, priest, rabbi, civil official)	
Special license	
Documents needed	
Attendants/participants	
Guest list	
Wedding present list	

Appendix 1

Clothes	
Rings	
Transport to/from wedding	
Photographer/video	
Invitations	
Service sheets	
Music	
Flowers	
Cake	
Catering	
Table plan	
Gifts for each other/attendants	
Honeymoon	

Appendix 2

Useful Addresses

American Humanist Association
P.O. Box 1188
Amherst, NY 14226-7188
(800) 743-6646

National Spiritualist Association of Churches
P.O. Box 217
Lily Dale, NY 14752-0217
(716) 595-2000

Quaker Information Center
1501 Cherry St.
Philadelphia, PA 19102
(215)-241-7024
quakerinfo@afsc.org
(include your mailing address in email requests)

United Fellowship of Metropolitan Community Churches
(800) 501-HOPE

Partners Task Force for Gay and Lesbian Couples
Box 9685
Seattle, WA 98101
(206)935-1206
demian@buddybuddy.com
www.buddybuddy.com

Focuses on legal issues surrounding gay and lesbian partnerships.

Appendix 3

Further Reading

Ceremonies of the Heart, Becky Butler (Seal Press, 1990).

Circles of Love, Rabbi Dr. Rudy Brasch (HarperCollins Australia, 1995).

Daring to Speak Love's Name, Elizabeth Stewart (Heinemann).

The Druid Way, Philip Carr Gomm (Element, 1993).

Emily Post on Second Weddings, Elizabeth L. Post (HarperPerennial, 1991).

Great Occasions, Andrew Hill, ed., (General Assembly of Unitarian Churches, 1992).

Marriage: A Fortress for Well-Being (The Baha'i Publishing Trust, 1973, 1988).

Marriage of Likeness: Same-Sex Unions in Pre-modern Europe, John Boswell (HarperCollins, 1995).

Poems of Love, Gail Harvey, ed., (Avenel Books, 1989).

Together Forever, Andrew Marshall (Cassells, 1995).

Further Reading

To Love and to Cherish, Jane Wynne Willson (British Humanist Association, 1988).

The Two of Us: Affirming, Celebrating and Symbolizing Gay and Lesbian Relationships, Larry J. Uhrig (Alyson Press, 1985).

Weddings from the Heart, Daphne Rose Kingma (Conari Press, 1991).

The Oxford Book of Marriage, Helge Rubenstein (Oxford University Press, 1992).

Index

161

Biblical extracts in readings, 41–42
Blessing
in Jewish weddings, 75
in religious blessing, 77–78, 79, 81
Blood test requirements, 19, 21
Board of good wishes, 55
Bondi, Herman, 123
Book of attendance, 55
Bouquet
flowers in, 35–36
throwing, 54–55
Bradford, Barbara Taylor, 11
Bride
handing over of, 6, 34–35, 69
special clothes for, 30–33
traditional presentation of, 68
Bride price in Viking wedding, 114
Brinkley, Christie, 144
British Gay and Lesbian Humanist Association (GALHA), 124–126
British Virgin Islands, wedding requirements in, 21
Buddhist ceremony, 8, 86–89
Butler, Becky, 135

C
Cake, wedding, 49–50
Candles
in pagan weddings, 97
in Rite of Holy Union ceremony, 123
Caribbean, wedding requirements in, 21
Catholic countries, 34
Celebrants, 19–20
in Baha'i wedding, 90–91
in Buddhist wedding, 87–89
choice of, 26–27
in civil ceremony, 19–20
in gay and lesbian ceremonies, 126–128, 130–133

in Humanist wedding, 110, 112, 113, 114
lack of, at Quaker wedding, 27, 74
in Las Vegas ceremonies, 147–149
in pagan wedding, 98, 99, 100–101
in religious blessing, 76–77, 78, 79, 81–83, 84–85
in Rite of Holy Union Christian service, 117–118, 119, 120, 121–122
in Spiritualist wedding, 94–95, 96
in traditional weddings, 26
Celebration, desire for, 7
Celebratory drinks, 48–49
Ceremonial Gongyo in Buddhist ceremony, 87
Ceremonies, 67
Baha'i, 89–93
basic format for, 67–68
in British Gay and Lesbian Humanist Association ceremony, 124–126
Buddhist, 86–89
civil, 19–20, 57, 58, 75–76
commitment, 11, 59, 62
Druid, 101–108
flowers at, 35–36
in gay and lesbian weddings, 58, 59, 116–143
Humanist, 57, 58, 59, 61, 62, 108–114, 124–126
interfaith, 85–86
Jewish, 75
legal requirements for, 19–21
music at, 36–40
need to personalize, 6–7
Pacifist, 57, 115
Pagan, 8, 58–59, 62, 97–100
Quaker, 73–74
readings at, 40–42

Index